Crochet Undercover

Quick-and-Easy Hats
for Your Little Superheroes

Cony Larsen

Design Originals

an Imprint of Fox Chapel Publishing
www.d-originals.com

Table of Contents

Introduction

I had so much fun creating the designs for **Crochet Undercover**. *From the time the concept began to dance around my head…to attaching the final touches to each hat…the only thing I could think about was how much fun each of my tiny heroes was going to have hiding their true identity under each hat.*

The patterns in **Crochet Undercover** *will complete whatever super-secret character your child wants to be for the day; whether they are ready to be the Superstar hero who saves the world from an evil nemesis, or the Mutant X ninja with super-cool karate moves, or the huge Dinomite that eats and destroys everything in its path—our hats are sure to please your pickiest heroes.*

Inside you will find a fabulous selection of children's one-of-a-kind hats, handcrafted with quality yarns in delicious designer colors. I'm sure you will enjoy making these as much as your superheroes will enjoy wearing them!

Cony Larsen
Author

BAT GIRL

Skill Level: Intermediate
Finished Size: 16½" in diameter 7½" from top to edge

Gauge: 6 sts=1", 8 rows=1"

Top Section
Ch 50,
Rnd 1 Sc in 2nd ch from hook, sc in next 47 ch, 3 sc in last ch, turn, sc in next 47 sts, 2 dc in last ch. Join with sl st to beg sc, (100 sts).
Rnd 2 Ch 1, sc in each st around. Join with sl st to beg sc, (100 sts).
Rnd 3–24 Ch 1, rep Rnd 2. Join with sl st to beg sc, (100 sts, 3").

Bat Silhouette
Bat silhouette is made with two bobbins of yellow yarn.
Attach one of the bobbins on Rnd 1 to start right wing. Attach second bobbin on Rnd 1 to start left wing. Use left bobbin to crochet all sts shaded gray. Use right bobbin to crochet all sts shaded yellow.
Rnd 1 Ch 1, sc in next 12 sts, pick up **right bobbin** and work sc in next 3 sts; pick up black yarn and work sc in next 20 sts; pick up **left bobbin** and work sc in next 3 sts; pick up black yarn and work sc in remaining sts. Join with sl st to beg sc, (100 sts).
Rnd 2–15 Ch 1, follow graph on page 5 to make bat silhouette, motif size is 6" w x 1⅝" h.

Lower Section
Rnd 1 Ch 1, sc in first st, sc in each st around. Join with sl st to beg sc, (100 sts).
Rnd 2–29 Rep Rnd 1, (100 sts, 7" from crown to edge).

Gauge
6 sts = 1"
8 Rows = 1"
Motif size is approximately:
6" X 1-7/8"

	1	17	16	15	14	13	12	11	10	9	8	7	6	5	4	3	2	1
	1	2	1		1	14	13	12	11		10	9	8	7	6	5	4	3	2	1
	4	3	2	1		14	13	12	11		10	9	8	7	6	5	4	3	2	1
	4	3	2	1		3	2	1		10	9	8	7	6	5	4	3	2	1
	8	7	6	5	4	3	2	1		10	9	8	7	6	5	4	3	2	1
	9	8	7	6	5	4	3	2	1		4	3	2	1	1	4	3	2	1
	10	9	8	7	6	5	4	3	2	1		2	1	2	1	4	3	2	1
	2	1	1	11	10	9	8	7	6	5	4	3	2	1	4	3	2	1
	2	1	2	1	10	9	8	7	6	5	4	3	2	1	4	3	2	1
	1	1	3	2	1	10	9	8	7	6	5	4	3	2	1	3	2	1
	6	5	4	3	2	1	12	11	10	9	8	7	6	5	4	3	2	1
	7	6	5	4	3	2	1	10	9	8	7	6	5	4	3	2	1	1
	8	7	6	5	4	3	2	1	8	7	6	5	4	3	2	1	2	1
	9	8	7	6	5	4	3	2	1	5	4	3	2	1	4	3	2	1
	10	9	8	7	6	5	4	3	2	1	3	2	1	5	4	3	2	1

Bat Silhouette has a total of 36 stitches across. White squares are scs in black yarn, yellow and gray squares are in yellow yarn.

Bat Silhouette is made with two bobbins of yellow yarn. Use one bobbin to crochet the yellow shaded squares and another bobbin to crochet the gray shaded squares.

Eye Section
Rnd 1 Ch 1, sc in next 10 sts (place a marker); sl st in next 12 sts (place marker); sc in next 6 sts (place marker); sl st in next 12 sts (place marker); sc in remaining sts. Join with sl st to beg sc, (100 sts).
Rnd 2 Ch 1, sc in next 10 sts, ch 18, sk next 12 sts; sc in next 6 sts, ch 18, sk next 12 sts, sc in remaining sts. Join with sl st to beg sc.
Rnd 3 Ch 1, sc in next 10 sts, *sk 1 ch, sc in 2nd ch, sc in next 15, sk last ch*, sc in 6 sts; rep from * to * once more, sc in remaining sts. Join with sl st to beg sc, (100 sts).
Rnd 4 Ch 1, sc in each st around. Join with sl st to beg sc, (100 sts).
Rnd 5 Ch 1, sc in next 9 sts, *2 sc dec in next 2 sts, sc in next 14 sts, 2 sc dec in next 2 sts*, sc in next 6 sts; rep from * to * once more; sc in remaining sts. Join with sl st to beg sc.
Rnd 6 Ch 1, sc in next 8 sts, *2 sc dec in next 2 sts, sc in next 12 sts, 2 sc dec in next 2 sts*, sc in next 6 sts; rep from * to * once more; sc in remaining sts. Join with sl st to beg sc.
Rnd 7 Ch 1, sc in next 7 sts, *2 sc dec in next 2 sts, sc in next 10 sts, 2 sc dec in next 2 sts*, sc in next 6 sts; rep from * to * once more; sc in remaining sts. Join with sl st to beg sc, (100 sts).
Rnd 8–9 Ch 1, sc in each st around. Join with sl st to beg sc.
Rnd 10 Ch 1, sl st in each st around. Join with sl st to beg sl st. You may fasten off at this point or crochet the Crab Stitch edging, see instructions below.

Crab Stitch Edging (optional)
Note: Usually you crochet from right to left, this edging is worked from left to right.
Rnd 1 Ch 1, *sc in the first st to your right and in each st around. Join with sl st to beg st. Fasten off. Weave in ends.

General Instructions
Hook Size: D/3 (3.25mm)
Materials: Cascade Heritage Sock Yarn #5601 Black 100gm/437yds.
Spud & Chloë Fine Sock Superwash Silk #7811 Bumble Bee 65gm/248yds.

DINOMITE BRONSON

Skill Level: Beginner
Finished Size: 19" in diameter 7¼" from top to edge.

Gauge: 6 sts =1", 6 rows=1"
Fits 1–3 years.

Top Section—Decagon Top

With Green Bean color yarn and hook B/1 (2.25mm), make a Magic Ring, see page 32.
Rnd 1 10 sc in *Magic Ring*. Join with sl st to beg sc, (10 sts).
Rnd 2 Ch 1, 2 sc in each sc around. Join with sl st to beg sc, (20 sts).
Rnd 3 Ch 1, sc in each st around. Join with sl st to beg sc, (20 sts).
Rnd 4 Ch 1, *sc in next st, 2 sc in next st*, rep from * to * around. Join with sl st to beg sc, (30 sts).
Rnd 5 Rep Rnd 3, (30 sts).
Rnd 6 Ch 1, *sc in next 2 sts, 2 sc in next st*, rep from * to * around. Join with sl st to beg sc, (40 sts).
Rnd 7 Ch 1, *sc in next 3 sts, 2 sc in next st*, rep from * to * around. Join with sl st to beg sc, (50 sts).
Rnd 8 Ch 1, *sc in next 4 sts, 2 sc in next st*, rep from * to * around. Join with sl st to beg sc, (60 sts).
Rnd 9 Rep Rnd 3, (60 sts, 4").
Rnd 10 Ch 1, *sc in next 5 sts, 2 sc in next st*, rep from * to * around. Join with sl st to beg sc, (70 sts, 4¼").
Rnd 11 Rep Rnd 3, (70 sts).
Rnd 12 Ch 1, *sc in next 6 sts, 2 sc in next st*, rep from * to * around. Join with sl st to beg sc, (80 sts, 5").
Rnd 13 Rep Rnd 3, (80 sts).
Rnd 14 Ch 1, *sc in next 7 sts, 2 sc in next st*, rep from * to * around. Join with sl st to beg sc, (90 sts, 5¾").
Rnd 15 Rep Rnd 3, (90 sts, 6").
Rnd 16 Ch 1, *sc in next 8 sts, 2 sc in next st*, rep from * to * around. Join with sl st to beg sc, (100 sts, 6¼").
If you wish to make a bigger hat you can add an extra rnd at this point; each rnd increases the size of the hat by 10 sts or approximately 1⅝". For making a smaller hat, see instructions on page 12.

Main Section

Change to hook C/2 (2.75mm).
Rnd 1 Ch 2, hdc in each st around. Join with sl st to beg st, (100 sts).
Rnd 2–17 Rep Rnd 1. Join with sl st to beg st, (100 sts, 4"). Fasten off. Set aside.

Ribbed Band

Ch 11 with hook C/2 (2.75mm),
Row 1 Sc in 2nd ch from hook, sc in each st across, ch 1 turn, (10 sts).
Row 2 Sc in Back Loop Only of each st across, ch 1 turn, (10 sts).
Row 3–100 Rep Rnd 2. Join band ends tog with sl st.
Row 101 Ch 1, work sc at the end of each row. Join with sl st to beg st, (100 sts).

Attaching Ribbed Band to Hat

Place band inside hat, with safety pins, secure band in place to avoid band from shifting.
Row 1 Ch 1, sc through both first sts from hat and band, sc in each st around. Join with sl st to beg sc, (100 sts). Fasten off. Weave in ends. Fold band to the outside.

Dino's Spikes (make 3)

With Cricket color yarn, make a Magic Ring, see page 32.
Rnd 1 8 sc in *Magic Ring*. Join with sl st to beg sc, (8 sts).
Rnd 2 Ch 1, 2 sc in first st, sc in next 3 sts, 2 sc in next st, sc in next 3 sts. Join with sl st to beg sc, (10 sts).
Rnd 3 Ch 1, 2 sc in first st, sc in next 4 sts, 2 sc in next st, sc in next 4 sts. Join with sl st to beg sc, (12 sts).
Rnd 4 Ch 1, 2 sc in first st, sc in next 5 sts, 2 sc in next st, sc in next 5 sts. Join with sl st to beg sc, (14 sts).
Rnd 5 Ch 1, 2 sc in first st, sc in next 6 sts, 2 sc in next st, sc in next 6 sts. Join with sl st to beg sc, (16 sts).
Rnd 6 Ch 1, 2 sc in first st, sc in next 7 sts, 2 sc in next st, sc in next 7 sts. Join with sl st to beg sc, (18 sts).
Rnd 7 Ch 1, 2 sc in first st, sc in next 8 sts, 2 sc in next st, sc in next 8 sts. Join with sl st to beg sc, (20 sts).
Rnd 8 Ch 1, 2 sc in first st, sc in next 9 sts, 2 sc in next st, sc in next 9 sts. Join with sl st to beg sc, (22 sts).
Rnd 9 Ch 1, 2 sc in first st, sc in next 10 sts, 2 sc in next st, sc in next 10 sts. Join with sl st to beg sc, (24 sts).
Rnd 10 Ch 1, 2 sc in first st, sc in next 11 sts, 2 sc in next st, sc in next 11 sts. Join with sl st to beg sc, (26 sts).
Rnd 11 Ch 1, sc in each st around. Join with sl st to beg sc. Fasten off leaving a 15" tail to sew in place.

Finishing Spikes

Block spikes before you get started, see page 15. Stuff spikes with fiberfill. Set aside.

(Continued on page 8)

DINOMITE BRONSON continued

Dino's Mouth

Ch 18 with Green Bean color yarn,

Rnd 1 Sc in 2nd ch from hook, sc in next 15 ch, 2 sc in last ch; turn, begin working other side of beg ch, sc in each ch across, sc in last ch. Join with sl st to beg st, (34 sts).

Rnd 2 Ch 1, sc in next 16 sts, 2 sc in next st; sc in next 16 sts, 2 sc in last st. Join with sl st to beg st, (36 sts).

Rnd 3 Ch 1, sc in next 17 sts, 2 sc in next st; sc in next 17 sts, 2 sc in last st. Join with sl st to beg st, (38 sts).

Rnd 4 Ch 1, sc in next 18 sts, 2 sc in next st; sc in next 18 sts, 2 sc in last st. Join with sl st to beg st, (40 sts).

Rnd 5 Ch 1, sc in next 19 sts, 2 sc in next st; sc in next 19 sts, 2 sc in last st. Join with sl st to beg st, (42 sts).

Rnd 6 Ch 1, sc in next 20 sts, 2 sc in next st; sc in next 20 sts, 2 sc in last st. Join with sl st to beg st, (44 sts).

Rnd 7 Ch 1, sc in next 21 sts, 2 sc in next st; sc in next 21 sts, 2 sc in last st. Join with sl st to beg st, (46 sts).

Rnd 8 Ch 1, sc in next 22 sts, 2 sc in next st; sc in next 22 sts, 2 sc in last st. Join with sl st to beg st, (48 sts).

Rnd 9 Ch 1, sc in next 23 sts, 2 sc in next st; sc in next 23 sts, 2 sc in last st. Join with sl st to beg st, (50 sts).

Rnd 10 Ch 1, sc in next 24 sts, 2 sc in next st; sc in next 24 sts, 2 sc in last st. Join with sl st to beg st, (52 sts).

Rnd 11 Ch 1, sc in each st around. Join with sl st to beg sc. (52 sts). Fasten off leaving a 24" tail to attach mouth to hat.

Finishing Mouth

Block mouth before you get started, see page 15. Set aside.

Dino's Teeth (make 7)

Ch 2 with hook size 5 (1.90mm) and DMC Crochet Cotton White,

Rnd 1 8 sc in 2nd ch from hook. Join with sl st to beg st, (8 sts).

Rnd 2 Ch 1, 2 sc in first st, sc in next 3 sts, 2 sc in next st, sc in next 3 sts. Join with sl st to beg sc, (10 sts).

Rnd 3 Ch 1, 2 sc in first st, sc in next 4 sts, 2 sc in next st, sc in next 4 sts. Join with sl st to beg sc, (12 sts).

Rnd 4 Ch 1, 2 sc in first st, sc in next 5 sts, 2 sc in next st, sc in next 5 sts. Join with sl st to beg sc, (14 sts).

Rnd 5 Ch 1, 2 sc in first st, sc in next 6 sts, 2 sc in next st, sc in next 6 sts. Join with sl st to beg sc, (16 sts).

Rnd 6 Ch 1, sc in each st around. Join with sl st to beg sc. Fasten off leaving a 12" tail to sew in place.

Finishing Teeth

Cut 7 teeth of Pellon Ultra Firm Stabilizer using pattern on page 38. Insert Stabilizer into teeth, with a tapestry needle and 12" tail, sew along open edge with whipstitch; leave remaining tail to sew in place. Block teeth, see page 15. Set aside.

Attaching Teeth to Mouth

Place teeth along the edge of mouth and secure in place with safety pins. With a tapestry needle and 12" tail sew teeth to mouth with whipstitch. Cut 2 pieces of Pellon Ultra Firm Stabilizer using pattern on page 38. Insert Stabilizer into mouth, with a tapestry needle and 24" tail, whipstitch open end of mouth together. Find center front of hat and match up with center of mouth, pin in place along sixth row up from bottom edge of main section of hat; whipstitch mouth to hat stitching through all thicknesses. Fasten off. Weave in ends.

Assembly

We used an 8" ball to hold hat in place; place hat over the ball, and use a fabric pencil to mark the placement for the mouth, nostrils and eyes. After you have marked the placement for the face, arrange face on hat and hold them in place with safety pins. Using whipstitch, sew mouth in place first; glue eyes with an extra strength glue; we used Amazing E-6000 Clear Waterproof Glue. Embroider nostrils or sew two ½" buttons for nostrils. Mark position of the spikes on the hat, the first spike should be sewn starting at the center top of hat and down toward the forehead. The second spike should be sewn 1" apart from the first spike going toward the back of the head, and the third spike should be sewn 1" down from second spike toward the back of the head.

General Instructions

Hook Size: B/1 (2.25mm) and C/2 (2.75mm); you will also need a steel hook size 5 (1.9mm).

Materials: Spud & Chloë Fine Sock Superwash yarn #7818 Green Bean 1 ball 65gm/248yds and 20 yards of #7804 Cricket. DMC Crochet Cotton #10 B5200 White.

Additional Supplies Needed: Two 1" round craft eyes and two ½" black buttons for nostrils. 6" of Pellon Single-Sided Fusible Lite-Weight Stabilizer for nose. Fabric pencil. Polyester Fiberfill. Tapestry needle.

TEMPEST

Skill Level: Beginner
Finished Size: 18" in diameter, 8" from top to bottom edge plus a 3" cuff.

Gauge: 5 sts=1", 4 rows=1"

Main Section
Ch 61,
Row 1 Sc in 2nd ch from hook, sc in each ch across, (60 sts).
Row 2 Ch 1, sc in **back loop only** of each sc across, (60 sts).
Row 3–92 Rep Row 2, join ends tog with sl st, (60 sts, 18" x 11½" finished size rectangle).
If you need to make a larger hat, you may add more rows. Each row increases the size of the hat by ¼".

Top
Rnd 1 Ch 1, sc at the end of first row, *ch 1, sk 1 row, sc at the end of next row*; rep from * to * around, (92 sts). Join with sl st to beg sc. Fasten off. Weave in ends.

Finishing Top
Cut a piece of same color yarn 24" long and fold in half; thread yarn through each ch-1 space, pull yarn to gather top closure, tie a double knot to secure knot. Decorate with a 3" white pom-pom.

General Instructions
Hook Size: E/4–3.5mm
Materials: Debbie Bliss Baby Cashmerino yarn #700 Ruby Red 2 balls each 50g/137yds, 50 yds White yarn for pom-pom.

9

FELINE HELIX

Skill Level: Beginner
Finished Size: 15½" in diameter 8¼" from top to edge.

Gauge: 6 sts =1", 6 rows=1"
Fits 1–3 years.

Top Section—Decagon Top

With Asphalt Gray color yarn and hook B/1 (2.25mm), make a Magic Ring, see page 32.
Rnd 1 10 sc in *Magic Ring*. Join with sl st to beg sc, (10 sts).
Rnd 2 Ch 1, 2 sc in each sc around. Join with sl st to beg sc, (20 sts).
Rnd 3 Ch 1, sc in each st around. Join with sl st to beg sc, (20 sts).
Rnd 4 Ch 1, *sc in next st, 2 sc in next st*, rep from * to * around. Join with sl st to beg sc, (30 sts).
Rnd 5 Rep Rnd 3, (30 sts).
Rnd 6 Ch 1, *sc in next 2 sts, 2 sc in next st*, rep from * to * around. Join with sl st to beg sc, (40 sts).
Rnd 7 Ch 1, *sc in next 3 sts, 2 sc in next st*, rep from * to * around. Join with sl st to beg sc, (50 sts).
Rnd 8 Ch 1, *sc in next 4 sts, 2 sc in next st*, rep from * to * around. Join with sl st to beg sc, (60 sts).
Rnd 9 Rep Rnd 3, (60 sts, 4").
Rnd 10 Ch 1, *sc in next 5 sts, 2 sc in next st*, rep from * to * around. Join with sl st to beg sc, (70 sts, 4¼").
Rnd 11 Rep Rnd 3, (70 sts).
Rnd 12 Ch 1, *sc in next 6 sts, 2 sc in next st*, rep from * to * around. Join with sl st to beg sc, (80 sts, 5").
Rnd 13 Rep Rnd 3, (80 sts).
Rnd 14 Ch 1, *sc in next 7 sts, 2 sc in next st*, rep from * to * around. Join with sl st to beg sc, (90 sts, 5¾").
Rnd 15 Rep Rnd 3, (90 sts, 6").
Rnd 16 Ch 1, *sc in next 8 sts, 2 sc in next st*, rep from * to * around. Join with sl st to beg sc, (100 sts, 6¼").
If you wish to make a bigger hat you can add an extra rnd at this point; each rnd increases the size of the hat by 10 sts or approximately 1⅝". For making a smaller hat, see instructions on page 12.

Main Section

Change to hook C/2 (2.75mm).
Rnd 1 Ch 1, sc in each st around. Join with sl st to beg sc, (100 sts).
Rnd 2–24 Rep Rnd 1. Join with sl st to beg sc, (100 sts, 4" from last inc rnd). Switch to White yarn color to start the Cuff.

Cuff Band

With White color yarn and hook B/1 (2.25mm),
Rnd 1 Ch 1, sc in each st around. Join with sl st to beg sc, ch 1, turn, inside of hat should be facing you, (100 sts).
Rnd 2 Sc in each st around. Join with sl st to beg sc, (100 sts).
Rnd 3–17 Ch 1, sc in each st around. Join with sl st to beg sc, (100 sts).
Rnd 18 Ch 1, *Crab Stitch* in each st around (see *Crab Stitch Instructions* on next column). Join with sl st to beg sc, (100 sts). Fasten off. Weave in ends.

Crab Stitch Edging (optional)

Note: Usually you crochet from right to left, this edging is worked from left to right.
Rnd 1 Ch 1, *sc in the first st to your right and in each st around. Join with sl st to beg st. Fasten off. Weave in ends.

Feline's Nose

Ch 4 with Pink color yarn and hook C/2 (2.75mm),
Rnd 1 2 sc in 2nd ch from hook, sc in next st, 3 sc in last ch, turn to work on opposite side of chs, sc in next 2 sts. Join with sl st to beg sc, (8 sts).
Rnd 2 Ch 1, 3 sc in 1st st, sc in next 3 sts, 3 sc in next st, sc in next 3 sts. Join with sl st to beg sc, (12 sts).
Rnd 3 Ch 1, sk first st, 3 sc in next st, sc in next 5 sts, 3 sc in next st, sk next st, sl st in next 3 sts. Join with sl st to beg ch. Fasten off and leave a 12" tail to sew in place.

Feline's Ears (make 2)

With Asphalt Gray color yarn, make a Magic Ring, see page 32.
Rnd 1 6 sc in *Magic Ring*. Join with sl st to beg sc, (6 sts).
Rnd 2 Ch 1, 3 sc in first st, sc in next 2 sts, 3 sc in next st, sc in next 2 sts. Join with sl st to beg sc, (10 sts).
Rnd 3 Ch 1, sc in each st around. Join with sl st to beg st, (10 sts).
Rnd 4 Ch 1, 3 sc in first st, sc in next 4 sts, 3 sc in next st, sc in next 4 sts. Join with sl st to beg st, (14 sts).
Rnd 5 Rep Rnd 3.
Rnd 6 Ch 1, 3 sc in first st, sc in next 6 sts, 3 sc in next st, sc in next 6 sts. Join with sl st to beg st, (18 sts).
Rnd 7 Rep Rnd 3.
Rnd 8 Ch 1, 3 sc in first st, sc in next 8 sts, 3 sc in next st, sc in next 8 sts. Join with sl st to beg st, (22 sts).
Rnd 9 Rep Rnd 3.
Rnd 10 Ch 1, 3 sc in first st, sc in next 10 sts, 3 sc in next st, sc in next 10 sts. Join with sl st to beg st, (26 sts).
Rnd 11 Rep Rnd 3.

(Continued on page 12)

Rnd 12 Ch 1, 3 sc in first st, sc in next 12 sts, 3 sc in next st, sc in next 12 sts. Join with sl st to beg st, (30 sts).

Rnd 13 Rep Rnd 3.

Rnd 14 Ch 1, 3 sc in first st, sc in next 14 sts, 3 sc in next st, sc in next 14 sts. Join with sl st to beg st, (34 sts).

Rnd 15 Rep Rnd 3. Join with sl st to beg st. Fasten off leaving a 12" tail to sew in place.

Finishing

Block ears, nose and hat before you get started, see page 15. Cut a piece of Pellon Stabilizer using pattern for ears and nose on page 39. Insert Stabilizer into ears; follow manufacturer's instructions to fuse Stabilizer to back of nose. Cut out Cat's Face pattern on page 39, cut mouth and nose out.

Assembly

We used an 8" ball to hold hat in place; place hat over the ball, place cut out paper pattern over the hat, with a fabric pencil mark the placement for the ears, nose, mouth and eyes. After you have marked the placement for the face, arrange face pieces on hat and hold them in place with safety pins. Sew eyes first, then sew nose in place with running stitch. Attach ears with running stitch.

To embroider mouth, thread needle with yarn doubled up to quadruple thickness of yarn; embroider using running stitch. Make a tassel for hair and secure at the top of hat.

General Instructions

Hook Size: B/1 (2.25mm) and size C/2 (2.75mm)

Materials: Cascade Heritage Sock Yarn #5631 Asphalt Gray 1 ball 100/gm–437/yds and #5682 White 10 yards, 5 yards of pink yarn. 5 yards of black yarn.

Additional Supplies Needed: Two ¼" round buttons for eyes. 3" of Pellon Single-Sided Fusible Lite-Weight Stabilizer for nose. Fabric pencil. Tapestry needle.

Adjusting the size of a hat

All of our hats are made in sections. The top section is usually a square, pentagon, hexagon, or decagon. A square top with four sides will increase each round by 4 stitches. A pentagon top with five sides will increase each round by 5 stitches. A hexagon top with six sides will increase each round by 6 stitches; and a decagon top with ten sides will increase each round by 10 stitches.

If you are crocheting a hat that uses a hexagon top, like Wind Warrior on page 34, you will notice that each round is done in increments of six stitches; starting with round 2 has 12 stitches, round 3 has 18 stitches, round 4 has 24 stitches, and so on. The gauge for Wind Warrior is 5 stitches=1", this means that with each round you are increasing the hat by a little over 1".

Using a little math to figure out your hat measurements

Measure your child's head. With a flexible measuring tape go around the head just above the eyebrows, just above the ears, down the back of the head where it meets the neck, and back to the center of the forehead. If your child's head measures 18", you need an 18" hat; your gauge is 5 sts=1". Now, multiply 18" x 5 sts: your hat hexagon top size needs to be 90 sts. This makes it simple to choose the size of your hat. If you want a bigger hat, you just need to add an extra round; if you want a smaller hat, you crochet one less round.

Will your finished hat measure up?

Keep your tension in check. Remember that your tension plays a big roll in the finished size of your hat. Make sure you've checked your gauge before you get started. If you are not achieving the pattern's specified gauge you can do a couple of things to correct it. First, you can change your hook size. A smaller size hook will make tighter stitches; a larger size hook will make bigger stitches. Second, your yarn can be changed. Thinner yarn will make smaller stitches; chunkier yarn will make bigger stitches.

★ ★

Cony's Tips
Tension, Tension, Tension

I cannot express how important tension is in crochet; it's the difference between 'handmade' and 'homemade'. If you crochet too tight, your project will curl up, if you crochet too loose, it will start to ruffle. Correct your tension by holding thread tighter or loosen up your thread hold. You can also switch your hook size to achieve the right gauge.

★ ★

FROSTBITE

Skill Level: Beginner
Finished Size: 16" in diameter 6½" from top to edge

Gauge: 5 sts =1", 7 rows=1"

Top Section—Decagon Top

With Black color yarn and hook B/1 (2.25mm), make a Magic Ring, see page 32.

Rnd 1 10 sc in *Magic Ring*. Join with sl st to beg sc, (10 sts).

Rnd 2 Ch 1, 2 sc in each sc around. Join with sl st to beg sc, (20 sts).

Rnd 3 Ch 1, sc in each st around. Join with sl st to beg sc, (20 sts).

Rnd 4 Ch 1, *sc in next st, 2 sc in next st*, rep from * to * around. Join with sl st to beg sc, (30 sts).

Rnd 5 Rep Rnd 3, (30 sts).

Rnd 6 Ch 1, *sc in next 2 sts, 2 sc in next st*, rep from * to * around. Join with sl st to beg sc, (40 sts).

Rnd 7 Ch 1, *sc in next 3 sts, 2 sc in next st*, rep from * to * around. Join with sl st to beg sc, (50 sts).

Rnd 8 Ch 1, *sc in next 4 sts, 2 sc in next st*, rep from * to * around. Join with sl st to beg sc, (60 sts).

Rnd 9 Rep Rnd 3, (60 sts, 4").

Rnd 10 Ch 1, *sc in next 5 sts, 2 sc in next st*, rep from * to * around. Join with sl st to beg sc, (70 sts, 4¼").

Rnd 11 Rep Rnd 3, (70 sts).

Rnd 12 Ch 1, *sc in next 6 sts, 2 sc in next st*, rep from * to * around. Join with sl st to beg sc, (80 sts, 5").

Rnd 13 Rep Rnd 3, (80 sts).

Rnd 14 Ch 1, *sc in next 7 sts, 2 sc in next st*, rep from * to * around. Join with sl st to beg sc, (90 sts, 5¾").

Rnd 15 Rep Rnd 3, (90 sts, 6").

Rnd 16 Ch 1, *sc in next 8 sts, 2 sc in next st*, rep from * to * around. Join with sl st to beg sc, (100 sts, 6¼").

If you wish to make a bigger hat you can add an extra rnd at this point; each rnd increases the size of the hat by 10 sts or approximately 1⅝". For making a smaller hat, see instructions on page 12.

Main Section

Change to hook C/2 (2.75mm).

Rnd 1 Ch 1, sc in each st around. Join with sl st to beg sc, (100 sts).

Rnd 2–28 Rep Rnd 1. Join with sl st to beg sc, (100 sts, 4" from last inc rnd).

Cuff Band

Rnd 1 Ch 1, sc in each st around. Join with sl st to beg sc, ch 1, turn, inside of hat should be facing you, (100 sts).

Rnd 2 Sc in each st around. Join with sl st to beg sc, (100 sts).

Rnd 3–14 Ch 1, sc in each st around. Join with sl st to beg sc, (100 sts).

Rnd 15 Ch 1, Crab Stitch in each st around (see *Crab Stitch* instructions on next column). Join with sl st to beg sc, (100 sts).

Crab Stitch Edging (optional)

Note: Usually you crochet from right to left, this edging is worked from left to right.

Rnd 1 Ch 1, *sc in the first st to your right and in each st around. Join with sl st to beg st. Fasten off. Weave in ends.

Frostbite's Eyes (make 2)

With Popcorn White color yarn, make a Magic Ring, see page 32.

Rnd 1 8 sc in *Magic Ring*. Join with sl st to beg sc, (8 sts).

Rnd 2 Ch 1, 2 sc in each st around. Join with sl st to beg sc, (16 sts).

Rnd 3 Ch 1, *sc in next st, 2 sc in next st*; rep from * to * around. Join with sl st to beg sc, (24 sts).

Rnd 4 Ch 1, *sc in next 2 sts, 2 sc in next st*; rep from * to * around. Join with sl st to beg sc, (32 sts).

Rnd 5 Ch 1, sc in each st around. Join with sl st to beg sc, (2" across). Fasten off leaving a 10" tail to sew in place.

Frostbite's Nose

With Bumble Bee color yarn, make a Magic Ring, see page 32.

Rnd 1 8 sc in *Magic Ring*. Join with sl st to beg sc, (8 sts).

Rnd 2 Ch 1, 2 sc in first st, sc in next 3 sts, 2 sc in next st, sc in next 3 sts. Join with sl st to beg sc, (10 sts).

Rnd 3 Ch 1, 2 sc in first st, sc in next 4 sts, 2 sc in next st, sc in next 4 sts. Join with sl st to beg sc, (12 sts).

Rnd 4 Ch 1, 2 sc in first st, sc in next 5 sts, 2 sc in next st, sc in next 5 sts. Join with sl st to beg sc, (14 sts).

Rnd 5 Ch 1, 2 sc in first st, sc in next 6 sts, 2 sc in next st, sc in next 6 sts. Join with sl st to beg sc, (16 sts).

Rnd 6 Ch 1, 2 sc in first st, sc in next 7 sts, 2 sc in next st, sc in next 7 sts. Join with sl st to beg sc, (18 sts).

Rnd 7 Ch 1, 2 sc in first st, sc in next 8 sts, 2 sc in next st, sc in next 8 sts. Join with sl st to beg sc, (20 sts).

Rnd 8 Ch 1, 2 sc in first st, sc in next 9 sts, 2 sc in next st, sc in next 9 sts. Join with sl st to beg sc, (22 sts).

Rnd 9 Ch 1, 2 sc in first st, sc in next 10 sts, 2 sc in next st, sc in next 10 sts. Join with sl st to beg sc, (24 sts).

Rnd 10 Ch 1, sc in each st around. Join with sl st to beg sc. Fasten off leaving a 12" tail to sew in place.

Finishing Nose

Cut a piece of Pellon Stabilizer using nose pattern on page 40. Insert Stabilizer into nose; with tapestry needle and 12" tail, sew along open edge with whipstitch. Set aside.

Frostbite's Feet (make 2)

With Bumble Bee color yarn, ch 7,

Rnd 1 Sc in second ch from hook, sc in next 2 sc, hdc in next 2 sc, 7 hdc in last ch, turn work and work on opposite side of chs, hdc in next 2 sc, sc in next 2 sc, 2 sc inc in last ch. Join with sl st to beg sc, (18 sts).

Rnd 2 Ch 1, 2 sc in first st, sc in next 4 sts, 2 hdc in each of next 7 sts, sc in next 5 sts, 2 sc in last st. Join with sl st to beg sc, (27 sts).

Rnd 3 Ch 1, 2 sc in first st, sc in next 6 sts, *sl st in next st, sk next st, 5 hdc in next st, sk next st*; rep from * to * two more times, sl st in next st, sc in next 6 sts, 2 sc in last st. Join with sl st to beg sc, (35 sts).

Rnd 4 Ch 1, 2 sc in first st, sc in next 7 sts, *sl st in next st, sc in next 5 sts*; rep from * to * two more times, sl st in next st, sc in next 7 sts, 2 sc in last st. Join with sl st to beg sc, (37 sts). Fasten off leaving a 20" tail to sew in place.

Assembly

Block all face pieces. Cut face pieces out of Pellon Stabilizer using the pattern pieces on page 40. Follow manufacturer's instructions to fuse Stabilizer to back of crocheted feet and eyes. Arrange face pieces on hat and hold them in place with safety pins. Sew eyes first and then feet in place with running stitch. Sew nose in place with whipstitch. Sew buttons for eyes. Block, see instructions below.

General Instructions

Hook Size: B/1 (2.25mm) and size C/2 (2.75mm)

Materials: Cascade Heritage Sock Yarn #5601 Black 1 ball 100/gm–437/yds and Spud & Chloë Fine Sock Superwash #7811 Bumble Bee 1 ball 54/gm–248/yds and #7800 Popcorn White 10 yards.

Additional Supplies Needed: Two ¼" buttons for eyes. 3" of Pellon Single-Sided Fusible Lite-Weight Stabilizer for feet and eyes. Tapestry needle.

Cony's Tips

Blocking

Always check the yarn label for any special care instructions. Many natural fibers, such as cotton, linen, and wool, respond well to steam blocking. However, you shouldn't use steam or heat on mohair or angora. Many acrylics and some blends shouldn't be blocked at all, especially with steam because they might melt. Use a hand towel or handkerchief and a padded ironing board. If you prefer, you can substitute a table or any flat surface that you have padded adequately.

Take the dampened towel or handkerchief, place it over the edge of the project, and steam with an iron holding slightly above finished project. Lift the towel and repeat with another section all the way around. Leave the item in place until it's dry.

ILLUSION

Skill Level: Beginner
Finished Size: 19" in diameter, 6½" from crown to edge, 8" across top.

Gauge: 5 sts=1", 5 rows=1"

Top Section – Hexagon Top

Make a Magic Ring, see page 32.
Rnd 1 9 sc in *Magic Ring*. Join with sl st to beg sc, (9 sts).
Rnd 2 Ch 1, 2 sc in each st. Join with sl st to beg sc, (18 sts).
Rnd 3 Ch 1, *2 sc in first st, sc in next 2 sts*; rep from * to * around. Join with sl st to beg sc, (24 sts).
Rnd 4 Ch 1, *2 sc in first st, sc in next 3 sts*; rep from * to * around. Join with sl st to beg sc, (30 sts).
Rnd 5 Ch 1, *2 sc in first st, sc in next 4 sts*; rep from * to * around. Join with sl st to beg sc, (36 sts, 2¼").
Rnd 6 Ch 1, *2 sc in first st, sc in next 5 sts*; rep from * to * around. Join with sl st to beg sc, (42 sts, 2½").
Rnd 7 Ch 1, *2 sc in first st, sc in next 6 sts*; rep from * to * around. Join with sl st to beg sc, (48 sts, 3").
Rnd 8 Ch 1, *2 sc in first st, sc in next 7 sts*; rep from * to * around. Join with sl st to beg sc, (54 sts, 3¼").
Rnd 9 Ch 1, *2 sc in first st, sc in next 8 sts*; rep from * to * around. Join with sl st to beg sc, (60 sts, 3½").
Rnd 10 Ch 1, *2 sc in first st, sc in next 9 sts*; rep from * to * around. Join with sl st to beg sc, (66 sts, 4").
Rnd 11 Ch 1, *2 sc in first st, sc in next 10 sts*; rep from * to * around. Join with sl st to beg sc, (72 sts, 4¼").
Rnd 12 Ch 1, *2 sc in first st, sc in next 11 sts*; rep from * to * around. Join with sl st to beg sc, (78 sts, 4¾").
Rnd 13 Ch 1, *2 sc in first st, sc in next 12 sts*; rep from * to * around. Join with sl st to beg sc, (84 sts, 5").
Rnd 14 Ch 1, *2 sc in first st, sc in next 13 sts*; rep from * to * around. Join with sl st to beg sc, (90 sts, 5½").
Rnd 15 Ch 1, *2 sc in first st, sc in next 14 sts*; rep from * to * around. Join with sl st to beg sc, (96 sts, 5¾").
Rnd 16 Ch 1, *2 sc in first st, sc in next 15 sts*; rep from * to * around. Join with sl st to beg sc, (102 sts, 6").
Rnd 17 Ch 1, *2 sc in first st, sc in next 16 sts*; rep from * to * around. Join with sl st to beg sc, (108 sts, 6½").
Rnd 18 Ch 1, *2 sc in first st, sc in next 17 sts*; rep from * to * around. Join with sl st to beg sc, (114 sts, 6¾").
Rnd 19 Ch 1, *2 sc in first st, sc in next 18 sts*; rep from * to * around. Join with sl st to beg sc, (120 sts, 7¼").
If you wish to make a bigger hat you can add an extra rnd at this point; each rnd increases the size of the hat by 6 sts or approximately 1⅛". For making a smaller hat, see instructions on page 12.

Main Section

Rnd 1 Ch 1, *2 sc in first st, sk next sc, sc in next 18 sts*; rep from * to * around. Join with sl st to beg sc, (120 sts).
Rnd 2–3 Rep Rnd 1. Join with sl st to beg sc, (120 sts).
Rnd 4 Ch 1, *2 sc in next st, sk next st, sc in next 17 sts, sk next st*; rep from * to * around, sk last st. Join with sl st to beg sc, (114 sts).
Rnd 5 Ch 1, *2 sc in first st, sk next st, sc in next 16 sts, sk next st*; rep from * to * around, sk last st. Join with sl st to beg sc, (108 sts).
Rnd 6 Ch 1, *2 sc in first st, sk next st, sc in next 15 sts, sk next st*; rep from * to * around, sk last st. Join with sl st to beg sc, (102 sts).
Rnd 7 Ch 1, *2 sc in first st, sk next st, sc in next 14 sts, sk next st*; rep from * to * around, sk last st. Join with sl st to beg sc, (96 sts).
Rnd 8 Ch 1, *2 sc in first st, sk next st, sc in next 13 sts, sk next st*; rep from * to * around, sk last st. Join with sl st to beg sc, (90 sts).
Rnd 9 Ch 1, *2 sc in first st, sk next sc, sc in next 13 sts*; rep from * to * around. Join with sl st to beg sc, (90 sts).
Rnd 10–12 Ch 1, sc in each st around. Join with sl st to beg sc, (90 sts).
Rnd 13 Ch 2, dc around **Back Post** of each sc around. Join with sl st to beg sc, (90 sts).
Rnd 14 Ch 1, sc around **Back Post** of each dc around. Join with sl st to beg sc, (90 sts). Fasten off. Weave in ends.

(Continued on page 18)

Cony's Tips
Mix 'n Match
Our hats are made of sections: the band, the main section, and the top section. You can mix and match the different bands, patterns, and tops from the different hats to suit your skill level. Stack the different sections to create your very own hat!

Front Visor

Row 1 Find the center back of your hat, sk the first 25 sts, join yarn in 26th st, sc in same st, sc around **front post** of next 38 sts, sc in next st, ch 1, turn, (40 sts).

Row 2 Sc in each st across, ch 2 turn, (40 sts).

Row 3 Sk 1st st, sc in next 6 sts, hdc in next 5 sts, *2 dc in next st, dc in next st*, rep from * to * 8 times, hdc in next 5 sts, sc in next 5 sts, 2 sc dec in next 2 sts, sl st in ch-2 space, ch 2, turn, (46 sts).

Row 4 Sk 1st st, sc in next 5 sts, hdc in next 5 sts, *dc in next 24 st, hdc in next 5 sts, sc in next 4 sts, 2 sc dec in next 2 sts, sl st in ch-2 space, ch 2, turn, (44 sts).

Row 5 Sk 1st st, sc in next 41 sts, 2 sc dec in next 2 sts, sl st in ch-2 space, ch 2, turn, (42 sts).

Row 6 Sk 1st st, sc in next 39 sts, 2 sc dec in next 2 sts, sl st in ch-2 space, ch 2, turn, (40 sts). Fasten off. Weave in ends.

Front Visor Underside

You may choose to leave the visor as a single layer, or you can make the underside to make it more sturdy.

Ch 41,

Row 1 Sc in second chain from hook, sc in each ch across, ch 2 turn, (40 sts).

Row 2 Sk 1st st, sc in next 6 sts, hdc in next 5 sts, *2 dc in next st, dc in next st*, rep from * to * 8 times, hdc in next 5 sts, sc in next 5 sts, 2 sc dec in next 2 sts, sl st in ch-2 space, ch 2, turn, (46 sts).

Row 3 Sk 1st st, sc in next 5 sts, hdc in next 5 sts, *dc in next 24 st, hdc in next 5 sts, sc in next 4 sts, 2 sc dec in next 2 sts, sl st in ch-2 space, ch 2, turn, (44 sts).

Row 4 Sk 1st st, sc in next 41 sts, 2 sc dec in next 2 sts, sl st in ch-2 space, ch 2, turn, (42 sts).

Row 5 Sk 1st st, sc in next 39 sts, 2 sc dec in next 2 sts, sl st in ch-2 space, ch 2, turn, (40 sts). Fasten off leaving a 24" yarn tail to stitch Front Visor Underside to Front Visor together.

Finishing

Block Front Visor, see page 15. Place Visor Underside over Front Visor aligning each stitch; use safety pins to hold the two sides together. With a tapestry needle and yarn, whipstitch visor together along the curved edge. Cut a piece of Pellon Stabilizer for visor using pattern on page 38. Insert Stabilizer between visor sides; whipstitch sides together along open edge.

General Instructions

Hook Size: E/4 (3.50mm)

Materials: Sublime Baby Cashmere Merino Silk DK #277 Tittlemouse 2 balls 51g/126yds.

Additional Supplies Needed: 10" of Pellon Single Sided Fusible Ultra Firm Stabilizer for visor.

★ ★ ★ ★ ★ ★ ★ ★ ★ ★ ★ ★ ★ ★ ★ ★ ★ ★ ★ ★

Cony's Tips
Practice

Practice makes perfect, but avoid perfection. However, the only way to correct your tension is to practice. After all is said and done, your crochet project exists ultimately to show your love for your family and friends. A simply decorated gift that features a beautiful edge is considered priceless. This is supposed to be fun! If you are not having fun, re-evaluate.

★ ★ ★ ★ ★ ★ ★ ★ ★ ★ ★ ★ ★ ★ ★ ★ ★ ★ ★ ★

IRON GIRL

Skill Level: Intermediate
Finished Size: 20" in diameter, 7 ½" from crown to edge; visor size 6 ½" w x 2"   Gauge: 6–7 sts=1" 6 rows=1"

To make our two-tone hat we used the *Hidden-Strand Method* to switch colors, see instructions on page 21.

Top Section – Square Top
With blue yarn, make a Magic Ring, see page 32.
Rnd 1 10 sc in *Magic Ring*. Join with sl st to beg sc, (10 sts).
Rnd 2 Ch 1, 2 sc in each st. Join with sl st to beg sc, (20 sts).
Rnd 3 Ch 1, *With blue yarn, sc in next 2 sts, 3 sc in next st, sc in next 2 sts. With red yarn, sc in next 2 sts, 3 sc in next st, sc in next 2 sts*, rep from * to * once more. Pick up blue yarn; join with sl st to beg sc, (28 sts).
Rnd 4 Ch 1, *With blue yarn, sc in next 3 sts, 3 sc in next st, sc in next 3 sts. With red yarn, sc in next 3 sts, 3 sc in next st, sc in next 3 sts*, rep from * to * once more. Pick up blue yarn; join with sl st to beg sc, (36 sts).
Rnd 5 Ch 1, *With blue yarn, sc in next 4 sts, 3 sc in next st, sc in next 4 sts. With red yarn, sc in next 4 sts, 3 sc in next st, sc in next 4 sts*, rep from * to * once more. Pick up blue yarn; join with sl st to beg sc, (44 sts).
Rnd 6 Ch 1, *With blue yarn, sc in next 5 sts, 3 sc in next st, sc in next 5 sts. With red yarn, sc in next 5 sts, 3 sc in next st, sc in next 5 sts*, rep from * to * once more. Pick up blue yarn; join with sl st to beg sc, (52 sts).
Rnd 7 Ch 1, *With blue yarn, sc in next 6 sts, 3 sc in next st, sc in next 6 sts. With red yarn, sc in next 6 sts, 3 sc in next st, sc in next 6 sts*, rep from * to * once more. Pick up blue yarn; join with sl st to beg sc, (60 sts).
Rnd 8 Ch 1, *With blue yarn, sc in next 7 sts, 3 sc in next st, sc in next 7 sts. With red yarn, sc in next 7 sts, 3 sc in next st, sc in next 7 sts*, rep from * to * once more. Pick up blue yarn; join with sl st to beg sc, (68 sts).
Rnd 9 Ch 1, *With blue yarn, sc in next 8 sts, 3 sc in next st, sc in next 8 sts. With red yarn, sc in next 8 sts, 3 sc in next st, sc in next 8 sts*, rep from * to * once more. Pick up blue yarn; join with sl st to beg sc, (76 sts).
Rnd 10 Ch 1, *With blue yarn, sc in next 9 sts, 3 sc in next st, sc in next 9 sts. With red yarn, sc in next 9 sts, 3 sc in next st, sc in next 9 sts*, rep from * to * once more. Pick up blue yarn; join with sl st to beg sc, (84 sts).
Rnd 11 Ch 1, *With blue yarn, sc in next 10 sts, 3 sc in next st, sc in next 10 sts. With red yarn, sc in next 10 sts, 3 sc in next st, sc in next 10 sts*, rep from * to * once more. Pick up blue yarn; join with sl st to beg sc, (92 sts).
Rnd 12 Ch 1, *With blue yarn, sc in next 11 sts, 3 sc in next st, sc in next 11 sts. With red yarn, sc in next 11 sts, 3 sc in next st, sc in next 11 sts*, rep from * to * once more. Pick up blue yarn; join with sl st to beg sc, (100 sts).

Rnd 13 Ch 1, *With blue yarn, sc in next 12 sts, 3 sc in next st, sc in next 12 sts. With red yarn, sc in next 12 sts, 3 sc in next st, sc in next 12 sts*, rep from * to * once more. Pick up blue yarn; join with sl st to beg sc, (108 sts).
Rnd 14 Ch 1, *With blue yarn, sc in next 13 sts, 3 sc in next st, sc in next 13 sts. With red yarn, sc in next 13 sts, 3 sc in next st, sc in next 13 sts*, rep from * to * once more. Pick up blue yarn; join with sl st to beg sc, (116 sts).
Rnd 15 Ch 1, *With blue yarn, sc in next 14 sts, 3 sc in next st, sc in next 14 sts. With red yarn, sc in next 14 sts, 3 sc in next st, sc in next 14 sts*, rep from * to * once more. Pick up blue yarn; join with sl st to beg sc, (124 sts).
If you wish to make a bigger hat you can add an extra rnd at this point; each rnd increases the size of the hat by 4 sts or approximately ⅝". For making a smaller hat, see instructions on page 12.

Main Section
With Dolphin Blue yarn,
Rnd 1 Ch 1, *sc in next 31 sts, with to red yarn, sc in next 31 sts,*. With blue yarn, rep from * to * once more. Pick up blue yarn; join with sl st to beg sc, (124 sts).
Rnd 2–24 Rep Rnd 1, (124 sts). Fasten off blue yarn.
Rnd 25 With red yarn, ch 1, sc in each st around, join with sl st to beg sc, (124 sts).
Rnd 26 Ch 2, dc around *Back Post* of each sc around. Join with sl st to beg sc, (124 sts).
Rnd 27 Ch 1, sc around **Back Post** of each dc around. Join with sl st to beg sc, (124 sts). Fasten off. Weave in ends.

Front Visor

With Red yarn,

Row 1 Find the center back of your hat, sk the first 22 sts, join yarn in 23rd st, sc in same st, sc around front post of next 48 sts, sc in next st, ch 1, turn, (50 sts).

Row 2 Sc in each st across, ch 2 turn, (50 sts).

Row 3 Sk 1st st, sc in next 6 sts, hdc in next 5 sts, *2 dc in next st, dc in next st*, rep from * to * 13 more times, hdc in next 5 sts, sc in next 5 sts, 2 sc dec in next 2 sts, sl st in ch-2 space, ch 2, turn, (64 sts).

Row 4 Sk 1st st, sc in next 5 sts, hdc in next 5 sts, dc in next 42 sts, hdc in next 5 sts, sc in next 4 sts, 2 sc dec in next 2 sts, sl st in ch-2 space, ch 2, turn, (62 sts).

Row 5 Sk 1st st, sc in next 4 sts, hdc in next 5 sts, dc in next 42 sts, hdc in next 5 sts, sc in next 3 sts, 2 sc dec in next 2 sts, sl st in ch-2 space, ch 2, turn, (60 sts).

Row 6 Sk 1st st, sc in next 57 sts, 2 sc dec in next 2 sts, sl st in ch-2 space, ch 2, turn, (58 sts).

Row 7 Sk 1st st, sc in next 55 sts, 2 sc dec in next 2 sts, sl st in ch-2 space, ch 2, turn, (56 sts).

Row 8 Sk 1st st, sc in next 53 sts, 2 sc dec in next 2 sts, sl st in ch-2 space, ch 2, turn, (54 sts).

Row 9 Sk 1st st, sc in next 51 sts, 2 sc dec in next 2 sts, sl st in ch-2 space, ch 2, turn, (52 sts).

Row 10 Sk 1st st, sc in next st, sc in st below from prior row across, sc dec in next 2 sts, sl st in ch-2 space, ch 2, turn, (50 sts). Fasten off.

Front Visor Underside

Ch 51,

Row 1 Sc in second chain from hook, sc in each ch across, ch 2 turn, (50 sts).

Row 2 Sc in each st across, ch 2 turn, (50 sts).

Row 3 Rep Rows 3–10 for *Front Visor*, (50 sts). Fasten off.

Finishing

Place Visor Underside over Front Visor aligning each stitch; use safety pins to hold the two sides together. With a tapestry needle and yarn, whipstitch visor together along the curved edge. Cut a piece of Pellon Stabilizer for visor using pattern on page 38. Insert Stabilizer between visor sides; whipstitch open side together along the edge of hat. Block visor, see page 15.

General Instructions

Hook Size: B/1 (2.25mm)

Materials: Spud & Chloë Fine Sock Superwash #7821 Dolphin Blue 65gm/248yds 1 ball, and Cascade Heritage Sock Yarn #5619 Red 100gm/437yds 1 ball.

Additional Supplies Needed: Three ¾" train buttons. 8" of Pellon Single-Sided Fusible Ultra Firm Stabilizer for visor. Tapestry needle.

Instructions: Read instructions for changing colors in the right column before you get started.

Hidden-Strand Method

In this traditional way of carrying two colors throughout a row, the strand not in use is hidden inside a single crochet, when you are ready to switch colors, pick up the hidden color as you would a new strand of yarn. One stitch before you want the new color to appear, drop the old color to the inside, along the top of the preceding row. Pick up the new color from the back as a yarn over, and draw it through the last two loops of the stitch. The next stitch will be the new color. This allows you to alternate two colors with no loose ends or strands in the middle of a row.

Inlay Method

Use this technique to make a color motif in one specific area (the eyes). Attach a bobbin or short strand of the new color where the motif begins. Use it for the motif stitches in each row. The background color floats behind the motif. The bobbin hangs behind the piece when the motif is not being worked. Keep bobbins closely wound to keep yarn from tangling when not in use. Catch up loose ends as you work other stitches, or weave in loose ends when you finish the work.

21

MUTANT X

Skill Level: Intermediate
Finished Size: 18" in diameter, 7¼" from top to edge plus a 1½" cuff.

Gauge: 5–6 sts=1", 6 rows=1"

Top Section—Decagon Top

With Snorkel color yarn, make a Magic Ring, see page 32.
Rnd 1 10 sc in *Magic Ring*. Join with sl st to beg sc.
Rnd 2 Ch 1, 2 sc in each sc around. Join with sl st to beg sc, (20 sts).
Rnd 3 Ch 1, sc in each st around. Join with sl st to beg sc, (20 sts).
Rnd 4 Ch 1, *sc in next sc, 2 sc in next sc* rep from * to * around. Join with sl st to beg sc, (30 sts).
Rnd 5 Rep Rnd 3. Join with sl st to beg sc, (30 sts, 2").
Rnd 6 Ch 1, *sc in next 2 sc, 2 sc in next sc* rep from * to * around. Join with sl st to beg sc, (40 sts).
Rnd 7 Ch 1, *sc in next 3 sc, 2 sc in next sc* rep from * to * around. Join with sl st to beg sc, (50 sts).
Rnd 8 Ch 1, *sc in next 4 sc, 2 sc in next sc* rep from * to * around. Join with sl st to beg sc, (60 sts).
Rnd 9 Rep Rnd 3. Join with sl st to beg sc, (60 sts, 3½").
Rnd 10 Ch 1, *sc in next 5 sc, 2 sc in next sc* rep from * to * around. Join with sl st to beg sc, (70 sts).
Rnd 11 Rep Rnd 3. Join with sl st to beg sc, (70 sts, 4").
Rnd 12 Ch 1, *sc in next 6 sc, 2 sc in next sc* rep from * to * around. Join with sl st to beg sc, (80 sts).
Rnd 13 Rep Rnd 3. Join with sl st to beg sc, (80 sts, 4½").
Rnd 14 Ch 1, *sc in next 7 sc, 2 sc in next sc* rep from * to * around. Join with sl st to beg sc, (90 sts).
Rnd 15 Rep Rnd 3. Join with sl st to beg sc, (90 sts, 5").
Rnd 16 Ch 1, *sc in next 8 sc, 2 sc in next sc* rep from * to * around. Join with sl st to beg sc, (100 sts, 5½").
If you wish to make a bigger hat you can add an extra rnd at this point; each rnd increases the size of the hat by 10 sts or approximately 1⅝". For making a smaller hat, see instructions on page 12.
Rnd 17–20 Ch 1, sc in each st around. Join with sl st to beg sc, (100 sts). Fasten off.

Eye Band Pattern (10 rnds, 2")

We used two techniques for switching colors for the Eye Band Pattern, the *Hidden-Strand Method* and the *Inlay Method*. See instructions on page 21. For the eyes, prepare two bobbins with 5 yards of Bumble Bee color yarn each.
Join Dachshund color yarn to Top Section's center back.
Rnd 1–2 Ch 1, sc in each st around. Join with sl st to beg sc, (100 sts).
Rnd 3–8 Work 6 rnds for Eye Band Pattern, see diagram on page 24. Switch yarn colors following instructions for *Hidden-Strand* and *Inlay Methods* on page 21.
Rnd 9–10 Ch 1, sc in each st around. Join with sl st to beg sc, (100 sts). Fasten off.

Main Section (16 rnds, 2½")

Join Snorkel color yarn,
Rnd 1–12 Ch 1, sc in each st around. Join with sl st to beg sc, (100 sts). Fasten off.

Ribbed Band

With Snorkel color yarn chain 11, turn.
Row 1 Sc in 2nd ch from hook and in each ch across, (10 sc) ch 1, turn.
Row 2 Sc in the back loop only of each sc across; (10 sc) ch 1, turn. Rep Row 2 until band reaches desired length, (100 rows). Join band ends tog with sl st.
Rnd 1 Ch 1, sc at the end of each row, (100 sc).

Attaching Ribbed Band to Main Section

Rnd 1 Place band inside hat's main section (wrong side of hat tog with right side of band), sl st through each sc (use back loops of band and front loops of hat only). Fasten off. Weave in all loose ends. Block.

Mutant X Ears (make 4)

With Snorkel color yarn, make a Magic Ring, see page 32.
Rnd 1 7 dc in *Magic Ring*, ch1, turn (7 sts).
Rnd 2 Sc in next 2 sts, *2 sc inc in next st*, rep from * to * 3 times, sc in next 2 sts, ch 1, turn, (10 sts).
Rnd 3 *Sc in next st, 2 sc inc in next st*, rep from * to * 4 times, sc in next 2 sts, ch 1, turn, (14 sts).
Rnd 4 Sc in each st. Fasten off leaving a 10" tail to sew in place.

(Continued on page 24)

Mutant X Hat
Eye Diagram

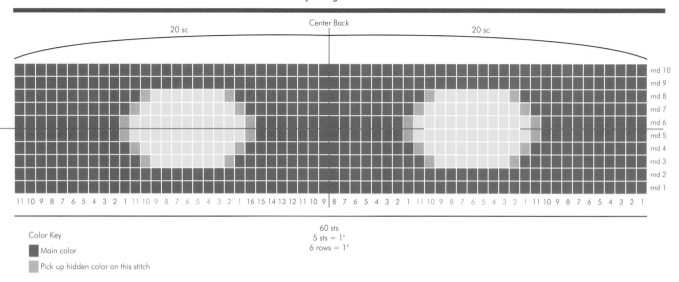

Color Key
◼ Main color
◻ Pick up hidden color on this stitch

60 sts
5 sts = 1"
6 rows = 1"

Finishing
Attach buttons to center of eyes and button for the nose.

General Instructions
Hook Size: B/1–2.25mm
Materials: Spud & Chloë Fine Sock Superwash 80% Wool-20% Silk yarn, #7809 Snorkel, #7803 Dachshund, and #7811 Bumble Bee, 1 ball each color 65/g each ball. Two ¼" buttons for eyes and a 1" button for nose.

★ ★ ★ ★ ★ ★ ★ ★ ★ ★ ★ ★ ★ ★ ★ ★ ★

Cony's Tips
DOs and DON'Ts
Keep it simple. Plan and read instructions before you get started. Go back and re-do if you are not pleased with the tension. Take a class to learn the basics. Keep your fibers protected in a yarn/thread dispenser while you work on your project. Don't wait for the perfect moment to get started.

★ ★ ★ ★ ★ ★ ★ ★ ★ ★ ★ ★ ★ ★ ★ ★ ★

ORSON LITTLE BEAR

Skill Level: Beginner
Finished Size: 19" in diameter 7½" from top to edge

Gauge: 5 sts=1"

Top Section—Decagon Top

Make a Magic Ring, see page 32.
Rnd 1 10 sc in *Magic Ring*. Join with sl st to beg sc, (10 sts).
Rnd 2 Ch 1, 2 sc in each sc around. Join with sl st to beg sc, (20 sts).
Rnd 3 Ch 1, sc in each st around. Join with sl st to beg sc, (20 sts).
Rnd 4 Ch 1, *sc in next st, 2 sc in next st*, rep from * to * around. Join with sl st to beg sc, (30 sts).
Rnd 5 Rep Rnd 3, (30 sts).
Rnd 6 Ch 1, *sc in next 2 sts, 2 sc in next st*, rep from * to * around. Join with sl st to beg sc, (40 sts).
Rnd 7 Ch 1, *sc in next 3 sts, 2 sc in next st*, rep from * to * around. Join with sl st to beg sc, (50 sts).
Rnd 8 Ch 1, *sc in next 4 sts, 2 sc in next st*, rep from * to * around. Join with sl st to beg sc, (60 sts).
Rnd 9 Rep Rnd 3, (60 sts, 4").
Rnd 10 Ch 1, *sc in next 5 sts, 2 sc in next st*, rep from * to * around. Join with sl st to beg sc, (70 sts, 4¼").
Rnd 11 Rep Rnd 3, (70 sts).
Rnd 12 Ch 1, *sc in next 6 sts, 2 sc in next st*, rep from * to * around. Join with sl st to beg sc, (80 sts, 5").
Rnd 13 Rep Rnd 3, (80 sts).
Rnd 14 Ch 1, *sc in next 7 sts, 2 sc in next st*, rep from * to * around. Join with sl st to beg sc, (90 sts, 5¾").
Rnd 15 Rep Rnd 3, (90 sts, 6").
Rnd 16 Ch 1, *sc in next 8 sts, 2 sc in next st*, rep from * to * around. Join with sl st to beg sc, (100 sts, 6¼").
Rnd 17 Ch 1, *Crab Stitch* in each st around (see *Crab Stitch* instructions below). Join with sl st to beg sc, (100 sts). Fasten off. Weave in ends.
If you wish to make a bigger hat you can add an extra rnd at this point; each rnd increases the size of the hat by 10 sts or approximately 2". For making a smaller hat, see instructions on page 12.

Crab Stitch Edging

Note: Usually you crochet from right to left, this edging is worked from left to right.
Rnd 1 Ch 1, *sc in the first st to your right and in each st around. Join with sl st to beg st.

Bear's Ears (make 4 halves)

With Light Tope color yarn, make a Magic Ring, see page 32.
Rnd 1 7 dc in *Magic Ring*, turn (7 sts).
Rnd 2 Ch 2 (counts as 1st dc), dc in 1st st, 2 dc in next 6 sts, turn, (14 sts).
Rnd 3 Ch 2 (counts as 1st dc), dc in 1st st, *dc in next st, 2 dc in next st*, rep from * to * around, end with dc in last st, turn, (21 sts).
Rnd 4 Ch 1, sc in each st. Fasten off leaving a 10" tail to sew in place.

Finishing Ears

With wrong sides together, align two ear halves, join together with sc. You may use a small piece of fiberfill to stuff the ears if desired. Attach ears to hat with a tapestry needle and whipstitch.

Bear's Nose

Make a Magic Ring, see page 32.
Rnd 1 8 sc in *Magic Ring*. Join with sl st to beg sc, (8 sts).
Rnd 2 Ch 1, 2 sc in each st around. Join with sl st to beg sc, (16 sts).
Rnd 3 Ch 1, sl st in 1st st, sc in next 8 sts, sl st in next st. Fasten off leaving a 10" tail to sew in place.

Bear's Snout

With Light Tope color yarn, make a Magic Ring, see page 32.
Rnd 1 6 Sc in *Magic Ring*. Join with sl st to beg sc, (6 sts).
Rnd 2 Ch 1, 2 sc in each st. Join with sl st to beg sc, (12 sts).
Rnd 3 Ch 1, *sc in next st, 2 sc in next st*; rep from * to * around. Join with sl st to beg sc, (18 sts).
Rnd 4 Ch 1, *sc in next 2 sts, 2 sc in next st*; rep from * to * around. Join with sl st to beg sc, (24 sts).
Rnd 5 Ch 1, *sc in next 3 sts, 2 sc in next st*; rep from * to * around. Join with sl st to beg sc, (30 sts).
Rnd 6 Ch 1, *sc in next 4 sts, 2 sc in next st*; rep from * to * around. Join with sl st to beg sc, (36 sts).
Rnd 7 Ch 1, *sc in next 5 sts, 2 sc in next st*; rep from * to * around. Join with sl st to beg sc, (42 sts).
Rnd 8 Ch 1, sc in each st around. Join with sl st to beg sc, (42 sts, 3" across). Fasten off leaving a 20" tail to sew in place.

Assembly

We used an 8" ball to hold hat in place; place hat over the ball, place cut out paper pattern from page 41 over the hat, with a fabric pencil mark the placement for the nose, snout, and eyes. After you have marked the placement for the face, arrange face on hat and hold them in place with safety pins. Using running stitch, sew nose onto snout first then sew ensemble onto hat. Sew eyes in place. Sew two ear halves together; you may use fiberbill to make ears more firm; mark position of the ears on the hat, with whipstitch sew ears to hat.

General Instructions

Hook Size: D/3 (3.25mm)
Materials: Debbie Bliss Baby Cashmerino #11 Chocolate 2 balls 50g/137yds, 10 yards of #48 Light Tope.
Additional Supplies Needed: Two ½" buttons for eyes. Tapestry needle.

STORM

STORM

Hat with Scarf

Skill Level: Beginner
Finished Size: 19" in diameter

Gauge: 5 sts=1"

Top Section – Hexagon Top

With Nutkin color yarn, make a Magic Ring, see page 32.
Rnd 1 6 Sc in *Magic Ring*. Join with sl st to beg sc, (6 sts).
Rnd 2 Ch 1, 2 sc in each st. Join with sl st to beg sc, (12 sts).
Rnd 3 Ch 1, *sc in next st, 2 sc in next st*; rep from * to * around. Join with sl st to beg sc, (18 sts).
Rnd 4 Ch 1, *sc in next 2 sts, 2 sc in next st*; rep from * to * around. Join with sl st to beg sc, (24 sts).
Rnd 5 Ch 1, *sc in next 3 sts, 2 sc in next st*; rep from * to * around. Join with sl st to beg sc, (30 sts).
Rnd 6 Ch 1, *sc in next 4 sts, 2 sc in next st*; rep from * to * around. Join with sl st to beg sc, (36 sts).
Rnd 7 Ch 1, *sc in next 5 sts, 2 sc in next st*; rep from * to * around. Join with sl st to beg sc, (42 sts).
Rnd 8 Ch 1, *sc in next 6 sts, 2 sc in next st*; rep from * to * around. Join with sl st to beg sc, (48 sts).
Switch to Muffin color,
Rnd 9 Ch 1, *sc in next st, sc in base of next st from Rnd 8*; rep from * to * around. Join with sl st to beg sc, (48 sts).
Rnd 10 Ch 1, *sc in next 7 sts, 2 sc in next st*; rep from * to * around. Join with sl st to beg sc, (54 sts).
Rnd 11 Ch 1, *sc in next 8 sts, 2 sc in next st*; rep from * to * around. Join with sl st to beg sc, (60 sts).
Rnd 12 Ch 1, *sc in next 9 sts, 2 sc in next st*; rep from * to * around. Join with sl st to beg sc, (66 sts).
Rnd 13 Ch 1, *sc in next 10 sts, 2 sc in next st*; rep from * to * around. Join with sl st to beg sc, (72 sts).
Rnd 14 Ch 1, *sc in next 11 sts, 2 sc in next st*; rep from * to * around. Join with sl st to beg sc, (78 sts).
Rnd 15 Ch 1, *sc in next 12 sts, 2 sc in next st*; rep from * to * around. Join with sl st to beg sc, (84 sts).
Rnd 16 Ch 1, *sc in next 13 sts, 2 sc in next st*; rep from * to * around. Join with sl st to beg sc, (90 sts, 6¼" circum).
If you wish to make a bigger hat you can add an extra rnd at this point; each rnd increases the size of the hat by 6 sts or approximately 1¼". For making a smaller hat, see instructions on page 12.

Main Section

Switch to Nutkin color,
Rnd 1 Ch 1, *sc in next st, sc in base of next st from Rnd 16*; rep from * to * around. Join with sl st to beg sc, (90 sts).
Rnd 2–8 Ch 1, sc in each st around. Join with sl st to beg sc, (90 sts).
Switch to Muffin color,
Rnd 9 Ch 1, *sc in next st, sc in base of next st from Rnd 8*; rep from * to * around. Join with sl st to beg sc, (90 sts).
Rnd 10–16 Ch 1, sc in each st around. Join with sl st to beg sc, (90 sts).

Switch to Nutkin color,
Rnd 17 Ch 1, *sc in next st, sc in base of next st from Rnd 16*; rep from * to * around. Join with sl st to beg sc, (90 sts).
Rnd 18–21 Ch 1, sc in each st around. Join with sl st to beg sc, (90 sts). Fasten off.

Ribbed Band

With Nutkin color, ch 11,
Row 1 Sl st in 2nd ch from hook, sl st in each ch across, ch 1 turn, (10 sts).
Row 2 Sl st in in each st across, ch 1 turn, (10 sts).
Row 3–66 Rep Row 2. Join ends tog with sl st, do not fasten off.
Row 67 Ch 1, sc in first st, sc 89 more sc evenly spaced around. Join with sl st to beg sc, (90 sts).

Attaching Ribbed Band to Hat

Place band inside hat, with safety pins, secure band in place to avoid band from shifting.
Row 1 Ch 1, sc through both first sts from hat and band, sc in each st around. Join with sl st to beg sc, (90 sts). Fasten off. Weave in ends. See directions for optional scarf below.

Scarf (make 2)

With Nutkin color, ch 21,
Row 1 Sl st in 2nd ch from hook, sl st in each ch across, ch 1 turn, (20 sts).
Row 2–20 Sl st in **Back Loop Only** of each st across, ch 1 turn.
Row 21 Sc in **Back Loop Only** of each st across, ch 1 turn.
Row 22–30 Rep Row 21, ch 1 turn.
Row 31 Sl st in **Back Loop Only** of each st across, ch 1 turn.
Row 32–50 Rep Row 31, ch 1 turn.
Switch to Muffin color,
Row 51 Ch 1 *sc in first st, sc in base of sc from Row 50*; rep from * to * across, ch 1 turn.
Row 52–60 Sc in **Back Loop Only** of each st across, ch 1 turn.
Row 61 Sl st in **Back Loop Only** of each st across, ch 1 turn.
Row 62–80 Rep Row 61, ch 1 turn.
Switch to Nutkin color,
Row 81 Ch 1, * sc in first st, sc in base of sc from Row 80*; rep from * to * across, ch 1 turn.
Row 82–90 Sc in **Back Loop Only** of each st across, ch 1 turn.
Fasten off leaving a 20" tail to attach scarf left side to hat.

Finishing

Find the center back of your hat, skip the first 12 sts to the right; with right sides tog attach scarf to hat with safety pins, using a tapestry needle and 20" tail, whipstitch scarf to the next 20 sc. Repeat with other side. Fasten off. Weave in ends.

Weave a piece of yarn through the sts at end of scarf, pull yarn to gather. Fasten off and weave in ends. You may choose to decorate the ends of your scarf with two crocheted balls or pom-poms. See instructions below.

Embellishing

Make a 3" pom-pom to decorate hat, attach to top of hat.

General Instructions

Hook Size: F/5 (3.75mm)
Materials: Sublime Baby Cashmere Merino Silk DK #278 Muffin and #275 Nutkin 50gm/126yds, two skeins of each color.

Crocheted Balls (optional)

Skill Level: Beginner
Finished Size: 7" in diameter
Gauge: 5 sts=1"
Hook Size: E/4 (3.50mm)

Balls are made from two halves sewn together. You can make balls in different colors or make them of a solid color, see instructions in right side column.

Crocheted Balls Instructions

Make 4 halves

With Nutkin color, make a Magic Ring, see page 32.
Rnd 1 6 sc in *Magic Ring*. Join with sl st.
Rnd 2 Ch 1, 2 sc in each st. Join with sl st, (12 sts).
Rnd 3 Ch 1, *1 sc in next st, 2 sc in next st*, rep from * to * around. Join with sl st to beg st, (18 sts).
Rnd 4 Ch 1, *1 sc in each of next 2 sts, 2 sc in next st*, rep from * to * around. Join with sl st to beg st, (24 sts).
Rnd 5 Ch 1, *1 sc in each of next 3 sts, 2 sc in next st*, rep from * to * around. Join with sl st to beg st, (30 sts).
Rnd 6 Ch 1, sc in each st around. Join with sl st to beg st, (30 sts).
Switch to Muffin color,
Rnd 7 Ch 1, sc in next st, sc in base of next st from Rnd 6*; rep from * to * around. Join with sl st to beg st, (30 sts).
Rnd 8 Ch 1, sc in each st around. Join with sl st to beg st, (30 sts).
Switch to Nutkin color,
Rnd 9 Ch 1, sc in each st around. Join with sl st to beg st, (30 sts). Fasten off leaving a 20" tail to sew both halves tog.

Finishing

With a tapestry needle and 20" tail, sew two halves tog with whipstitch, leaving a 1" opening to fill ball with fiberfill, whipstitch to the end. Fasten off. Weave in ends.

Attaching Ball to Scarf

We attached a ½" button to the ball, then gathered scarf end around button. Block entire project, see page 15.

Materials: Sublime Baby Cashmere Merino Silk DK #278 Muffin and #275 Nutkin 50gm/126yds, one skein of each color. Use the leftover yarn from hat to make balls. Fiberfill to fill squishy balls.

SUPER STAR

Skill Level: Beginner
Finished Size: 19" in diameter 8¼" from top to edge, plus a 1¾" cuff.

Gauge: 6 sts =1", 6 rows=1"
Fits 6–8 years.

Top Section—Decagon Top

Make a Magic Ring, see page 32.

Rnd 1 10 sc in *Magic Ring*. Join with sl st to beg sc, (10 sts).

Rnd 2 Ch 1, 2 sc in each sc around. Join with sl st to beg sc, (20 sts).

Rnd 3 Ch 1, sc in each st around. Join with sl st to beg sc, (20 sts).

Rnd 4 Ch 1, *sc in next st, 2 sc in next st*, rep from * to * around. Join with sl st to beg sc, (30 sts).

Rnd 5 Rep Rnd 3, (30 sts).

Rnd 6 Ch 1, *sc in next 2 sts, 2 sc in next st*, rep from * to * around. Join with sl st to beg sc, (40 sts).

Rnd 7 Rep Rnd 3, (40 sts).

Rnd 8 Ch 1, *sc in next 3 sts, 2 sc in next st*, rep from * to * around. Join with sl st to beg sc, (50 sts).

Rnd 9 Rep Rnd 3, (50 sts).

Rnd 10 Ch 1, *sc in next 4 sts, 2 sc in next st*, rep from * to * around. Join with sl st to beg sc, (60 sts).

Rnd 11 Rep Rnd 3, (60 sts, 4").

Rnd 12 Ch 1, *sc in next 5 sts, 2 sc in next st*, rep from * to * around. Join with sl st to beg sc, (70 sts, 4¼").

Rnd 13 Rep Rnd 3, (70 sts).

Rnd 14 Ch 1, *sc in next 6 sts, 2 sc in next st*, rep from * to * around. Join with sl st to beg sc, (80 sts, 5").

Rnd 15 Rep Rnd 3, (80 sts).

Rnd 16 Ch 1, *sc in next 7 sts, 2 sc in next st*, rep from * to * around. Join with sl st to beg sc, (90 sts, 5¾").

Rnd 17 Rep Rnd 3, (90 sts, 6").

Rnd 18 Ch 1, *sc in next 8 sts, 2 sc in next st*, rep from * to * around. Join with sl st to beg sc, (100 sts, 6¼").

If you wish to make a bigger hat you can add an extra rnd at this point; each increase rnd increases the size of the hat by 10 sts or approximately 1⅝". For making a smaller hat, see instructions on page 12.

Main Section

Rnd 1 Ch 1, sc in next 9 sts, sc in **Back Loop Only** of next st*; rep from * to * 9 more times. Join with sl st to beg st, (100 sts).

Rnd 2–20 Rep Rnd 1. Join with sl st to beg st, (100 sts, 4" from last inc rnd). Fasten off.

Eye Section

Rnd 1 Ch 1, sc in next 35 sts (place a marker); sl st in next 12 sts (place marker); sc in next 6 sts (place marker); sl st in next 12 sts (place marker); sc in remaining 35 sts. Join with sl st to beg sc, (100 sts).

Rnd 2 Ch 1, sc in next 35 sts, ch 18, sk next 12 sts; sc in next 6 sts, ch 18, sk next 12 sts, sc in remaining 35 sts. Join with sl st to beg sc.

Rnd 3 Ch 1, sc in next 35 sts, *sk 1 ch, sl st in 2nd ch, sl st in next 15 sts, sk last ch*, sc in 6 sts; rep from * to * once more, sc in remaining 35 sts. Join with sl st to beg st.

Rnd 4 Ch 1, sc in next 35 sts, *sk 1 st, sl st in next st, sl st in next 14 sts, sk last ch*, sc in 6 sts; rep from * to * once more, sc in remaining 35 sts. Join with sl st to beg st.

Rnd 5 Ch 1, sc in next 35 sts, *sk 1 st, sl st in next st, sl st in next 12 sts, sk last ch*, sc in 6 sts; rep from * to * once more, sc in remaining 35 sts. Join with sl st to beg st, (100 sts)

Rnd 6–7 Ch 1, sc in each st around. Join with sl st to beg st, ch 1, turn, inside of hat is now facing you, (100 sts).

Cuff Band

Row 1 Sc in each st around. Join with sl st to beg st, (100 sts).

Row 2–10 Ch 1, sc in each st around. Join with sl st to beg st, (100 sts).

Row 11 Ch 1, sl st in each st around. Join with sl st to beg st, (100 sts). Fasten off. Weave in ends.

Pentagon Shield

With #7821 Dolphin Blue color yarn, make a Magic Ring, see page 32.

Rnd 1 10 sc in *Magic Ring*. Join with sl st to beg st, (10 sts).

Rnd 2 Ch 1, 2 sc in each st around. Join with sl st to beg st, (20 sts).

Rnd 3 Ch 1, *sc in next 3 sts, 2 sc in next st*, rep from * to * around. Join with sl st to beg st, (25 sts).

Rnd 4 Ch 1, sc in next 3 sts, *sk next st, 3 sc in next st, sc in next 3 sts*, rep from * to * around. Join with sl st to beg st, (30 sts).

Rnd 5 Ch 1, sc in next 4 sts, *2 sc in next st, sc in next 5 sts, rep from * to * around, end with sc in last st. Join with sl st to beg st, (35 sts).

Rnd 6 Ch 1, sc in next 4 sts, *sk next st, 3 sc in next st, sc in next 5 sts*, rep from * to * around, end with sc in last st. Join with sl st to beg st, (40 sts).

Rnd 7 Ch 1, sc in next 5 sts, *2 sc in next st, sc in next 7 sts, rep from * to * around, end with sc in last 2 sts. Join with sl st to beg st, (45 sts).

Rnd 8 Ch 1, sc in next 5 sts, *sk next st, 3 sc in next st, sc in next 7 sts*, rep from * to * around, end with sc in last 2 sts. Join with sl st to beg st, (50 sts).

Rnd 9 Ch 1, sc in next 6 sts, *2 sc in next st, sc in next 9 sts, rep from * to * around, end with sc in last 3 sts. Join with sl st to beg st, (55 sts).

(Continued on page 32)

Rnd 10 Ch 1, sc in next 6 sts, *sk next st, 3 sc in next st, sc in next 9 sts*, rep from * to * around, end with sc in last 3 sts. Join with sl st to beg st, (60 sts).
Switch to #7800 Popcorn color yarn,
Rnd 11 Ch 1, sc in next 7 sts, *2 sc in next st, sc in next 11 sts, rep from * to * around, end with sc in last 4 sts. Join with sl st to beg st, (65 sts). Fasten off leaving a 24" yarn tail to attach shield to hat.

Felt Stars

Cut two squares of wool felt and Pellon Stabilizer using pattern on page 38. Follow manufacturer's instructions to fuse Stabilizer to back of the wool felt. After fusing stabilizer to wool felt, trace the star's pattern on page 38 onto the wool felt with a fabric pencil and cut stars. Place a dot of glue on the back of small star and secure onto large star. With matching color thread, make a small stitch on each point of the small star to secure to large star. Secure large star to pentagon with safety pins. Place a dot of glue on the back center of large star and secure onto pentagon shield. With matching color thread, make a small stitch on each point of the large star to secure ensemble onto pentagon.

Finishing Shield

Arrange shield as shown on hat and hold in place with safety pins. Sew shield onto hat with 24" yarn tail using running stitch. Fasten off. Weave in ends.
Note: you may glue the star ensemble together and then glue the shield to the hat instead of sewing pieces together. Block.

General Instructions

Hook Size: D/3 (3.25mm)
Materials: Debbie Bliss Baby Cashmerino yarn 2 skeins color #34 Cherry 50gm/137yds, 20 yards of #7821 Dolphin Blue, 2 yards of #7800 Popcorn (you may use any type of yarn you might have in your stash if you don't want to purchase extra yarn for the shield).
Additional Supplies Needed: Red and white 100% Wool Felt. 6" of Pellon Single-Sided Fusible Lite-Weight Stabilizer for stars.

Magic Ring

A magic ring, also know as an adjustable ring or magic circle loop. is a starting technique for crocheting in rounds by creating a loop that allows you to put the stitches in; you can then draw up tight the loop to leave no visible hole in the center.

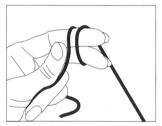

1) Leaving a 10" tail, wind the yarn from the yarn ball around your fingers as shown.

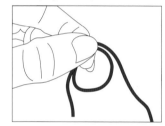

2) Grasp the yarn at the top where the strands overlap.

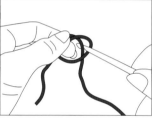

3) Insert hook through the front of the ring and grab the yarn.

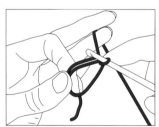

4) Pull up a loop.

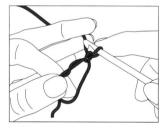

5) Chain 1, this chain is to "lock" the magic ring, it is not part of your stitch count. You may pull on the yarn to tighten the lock.

6) Chain 1, *insert hook through ring, yarn over, and pull through both loops on hook*, single crochet made, repeat from * to * to make as many single crochets as the pattern requires.

7) After completing the number of stitches in the ring: grab the tail and pull firmly to close the ring.

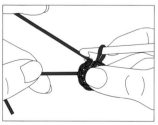

8) Join ring with slip stitch by inserting hook through both loops of beginning single crochet (see pink arrow); don't insert hook through beginning "lock" stitch. Pull the tail again tightly to close center completely.

WIND WARRIOR

Skill Level: Beginner
Finished Size: 19" in diameter 7" from crown to bottom edge.

Gauge: 5 sts=1", 5 rows=1"

Top Section—Hexagon Top

With Tittlemouse color, make a Magic Ring, see page 32.

Rnd 1 6 Sc in *Magic Ring*. Join with sl st to beg sc, (6 sts).

Rnd 2 Ch 1, 2 sc in each st. Join with sl st to beg sc, (12 sts).

Rnd 3 Ch 1, *sc in next st, 2 sc in next st*; rep from * to * around. Join with sl st to beg sc, (18 sts).

Rnd 4 Ch 1, *sc in next 2 sts, 2 sc in next st*; rep from * to * around. Join with sl st to beg sc, (24 sts).

Rnd 5 Ch 1, *sc in next 3 sts, 2 sc in next st*; rep from * to * around. Join with sl st to beg sc, (30 sts).

Rnd 6 Ch 1, *sc in next 4 sts, 2 sc in next st*; rep from * to * around. Join with sl st to beg sc, (36 sts).

Rnd 7 Ch 1, *sc in next 5 sts, 2 sc in next st*; rep from * to * around. Join with sl st to beg sc, (42 sts).

Switch to Skipper color,

Rnd 8 Ch 1, *sc in next 6 sts, 2 sc in next st*; rep from * to * around. Join with sl st to beg sc, (48 sts).

Rnd 9 Ch 1, *sc in next 7 sts, 2 sc in next st*; rep from * to * around. Join with sl st to beg sc, (54 sts).

Rnd 10 Ch 1, *sc in next 8 sts, 2 sc in next st*; rep from * to * around. Join with sl st to beg sc, (60 sts).

Rnd 11 Ch 1, *sc in next 9 sts, 2 sc in next st*; rep from * to * around. Join with sl st to beg sc, (66 sts).

Rnd 12 Ch 1, *sc in next 10 sts, 2 sc in next st*; rep from * to * around. Join with sl st to beg sc, (72 sts).

Rnd 13 Ch 1, *sc in next 11 sts, 2 sc in next st*; rep from * to * around. Join with sl st to beg sc, (78 sts).

Rnd 14 Ch 1, *sc in next 12 sts, 2 sc in next st*; rep from * to * around. Join with sl st to beg sc, (84 sts).

Switch to Water Lilly color,

Rnd 15 Ch 1, *sc in next 12 sts, 2 sc in next st*; rep from * to * around. Join with sl st to beg sc, (90 sts, 6¼" circum).

If you wish to make a bigger hat you can add an extra rnd at this point, each round increases the size of the hat by approximately 1".

If you wish to make a bigger hat you can add an extra rnd at this point; each rnd increases the size of the hat by 6 sts or approximately 1¼". For making a smaller hat, see instructions on page 12.

Main Section

With Water Lilly color,

Rnd 1–6 Ch 1, sc in in each st around. Join with sl st to beg sc, (90 sts).

Switch to Tittlemouse color,

Rnd 1–7 Ch 1, work 7 rounds of sc in each st around. Join with sl st to beg sc, (90 sts).

Switch to Skipper color,

Rnd 1 Ch 1, *sc in next st, sc in base of next st from Rnd 7*; rep from * to * around. Join with sl st to beg sc, (90 sts).

Rnd 2–7 Ch 1, work 6 rounds of sc in each st around. Join with sl st to beg sc, (90 sts).

Switch to Water Lilly color,

Rnd 1 Ch 1, *sc in next st, sc in base of next st from Rnd 7*; rep from * to * around. Join with sl st to beg sc, (90 sts).

Rnd 2 Ch 1, sc in each st around. Join with sl st to beg sc, (90 sts).

Front Flap

With Water Lilly color,

Row 1 Find the center back of your hat, sk the first 28 sts, join Water Lilly color in 29th st, sc in same st, sc **around front post** of next 38 sts, ch 1, turn, (40 sts).

Row 2–6 Sc in each st across, ch 1 turn, (40 sts).

Row 7 Sc in next 38 sts, 2 sc dec in last 2 sts, ch 1, turn, (39 sts).

Row 8 Sc in next 37 sts, 2 sc dec in last 2 sts, ch 1, turn, (38 sts).

Row 9 Sc in next 36 sts, 2 sc dec in last 2 sts, ch 1, turn, (37 sts).

Row 10 Sc in next 35 sts, 2 sc dec in last 2 sts, ch 1, turn, (36 sts).

Row 11 Sc in next 34 sts, 2 sc dec in last 2 sts, ch 1, turn, (35 sts).

Row 12 2 sc dec in next 2 sts, sc in next 31 sts, 2 sc dec in last 2 sts, ch 1, turn, (33 sts).

Row 13 Rep Row 12, ch 1, turn, (31 sts). Fasten off. Weave in ends.

Left Side Ear Flap

With Tittlemouse color,

Row 1 Join Tittlemouse color in st next to **left side base of the Front Flap**, sc in same st, sc in next 13 sts, ch 1, turn, (14 sts).

Row 2–8 Sc in each st across, ch 1 turn, (14 sts).

Row 9 2 sc dec in next 2 sts, sc in next 10 sts, 2 sc dec in last 2 sts, ch 1, turn, (12 sts).

Row 10 2 sc dec in next 2 sts, sc in next 8 sts, 2 sc dec in last 2 sts, ch 1, turn, (10 sts).

Row 11 2 sc dec in next 2 sts, sc in next 6 sts, 2 sc dec in last 2 sts, ch 1, turn, (8 sts).

Row 12 2 sc dec in next 2 sts, sc in next 4 sts, 2 sc dec in last 2 sts, ch 1, turn, (6 sts).

Row 13 2 sc dec in next 2 sts, sc in next 2 sts, 2 sc dec in last 2 sts, ch 1, turn, (4 sts). Fasten off. Weave in ends.

Right Side Ear Flap

With Tittlemouse color,

Row 1 Find the center back of your hat, sk the first 10 sts, join Tittlemouse color in 11th st, sc in same st, sc in next 13 sts, ch 1, turn, (your 14th st should be next to the st where your Front Flap begins), (14 sts).

Row 2–13 Rep Rows 2–13 for Left Side Ear Flap. Fasten off. Weave in ends.

Front Flap Crab Stitch Edging

With Water Lilly color,

Fold flap up towards the hat, with flap facing you, join yarn at the base of left side of flap; *crochet stitches to the right*, ch 1, sc along left side of flap evenly spaced, sc across top edge of flap, sc along right side of flap evenly spaced. Fasten off. Weave in ends.

With Tittlemouse color,

Join yarn **at the base of Left Ear Flap** Crab Stitch Edging,

Rnd 1 Ch 1, sc along the side of Left Ear Flap evenly spaced, sc across top edge of left Ear Flap, sc along the side of left Ear Flap evenly spaced, sc across back of neck, sc around Right Ear Flap.

Rnd 2 Crab Stitch Edging, *crochet stitches to the right*, ch 1, sc to the right around right Ear Flap, sc along the back of neck, sc along left Ear Flap. Fasten off. Weave in ends.

Right Side Strap

With Tittlemouse color, ch 6,

Row 1 Sl st in 2nd ch from hook, ch 1 turn, (5 sts).

Row 2–60 Sl st in **back loop only** of each st, ch 1, turn (5 sts). Buttonhole

Row 61 Sl st in next 2 sts, ch 3, sk st, sl st in next 2 sts, ch 1, turn (7 sts).

Row 62 Sl st in next 2 sts, sl st in ch 3 space, sl st in last 2 sts, ch 1, turn (5 sts).

Row 63–64 Sl st in each st across. Fasten off leaving a 12" tail to sew in place.

Finishing Right Side Strap

Attach strap to Right Ear Flap with running stitch. Sew buttons in place about ½" apart from each other, placing first button 3" from end of strap.

Left Side Strap

With Tittlemouse color, ch 6,

Row 1 Sl st in 2nd ch from hook, ch 1 turn, (5 sts).

Row 2–16 Sl st in **back loop only** of each st, ch 1, turn. Fasten off leaving a 12" tail to sew in place.

Finishing Left Side Strap

Slip D ring through left side strap, fold in half, whipstitch ends together, attach strap to Left Ear Flap with running stitch. Fasten off.

Finishing Hat

Fold flap up towards hat, secure in place with safety pins at each corner, with a fabric pen, mark the position for star buttons; sew buttons in place, sew through all thickness. Block entire project, see page 15.

General Instructions

Hook Size: F/5 (3.75mm)

Materials: Sublime Baby Cashmere Merino Silk DK 1 skein each #277 Tittlemouse, #5 Water Lilly, and #276 Skipper 50gm/126yds.

Additional Supplies Needed: One ½" D ring, three ½" buttons, and two ½" metal star buttons.

Stitch Guide

Holding the hook

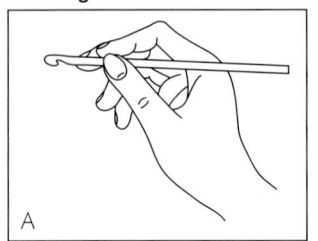

A

B

Holding the yarn

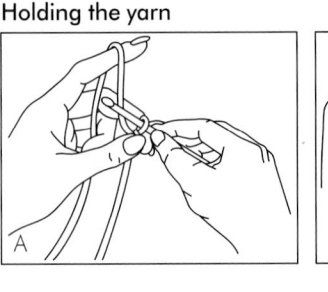

A

B

Slip knot

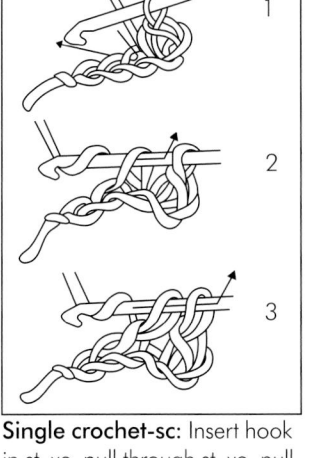

Start with a slip knot on your hook.

Yarn over

Yarn over-yo: Yarn over (yo), pull through loop (lp) on hook.

Chain

Chain-ch: Yarn over (yo), pull through loop (lp) on hook.

Slip stitch

Slip stitch-sl st: Insert hook in st, pull through both loops on hook.

Single crochet

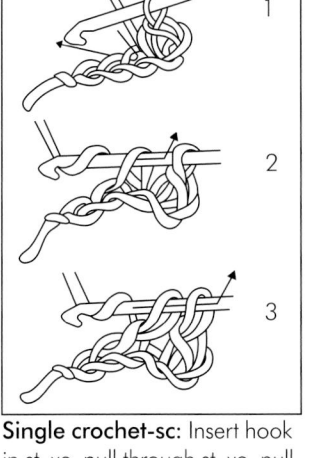

1

2

3

Single crochet-sc: Insert hook in st, yo, pull through st, yo, pull through both loops on hook.

Half double crochet

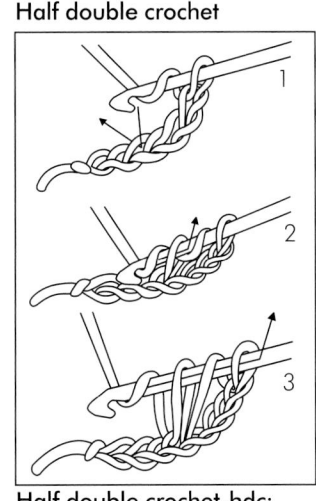

1

2

3

Half double crochet-hdc: Yo, insert hook in st, yo, pull through st, yo pull through all 3 loops on hook.

Double Crochet

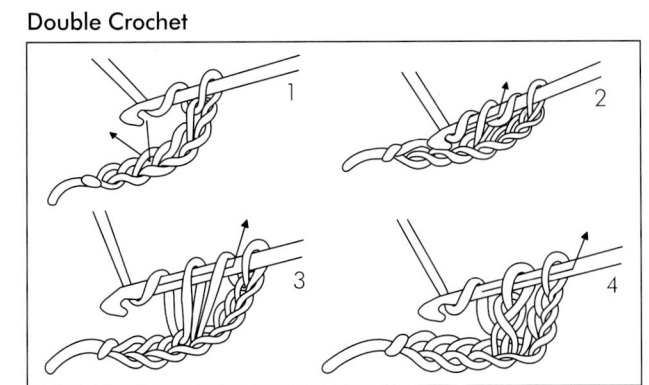

1

2

3

4

Double Crochet-dc: Yo, insert hook in st, yo, pull through st, [yo, pull through 2 lps] twice.

Front loop–Back loop

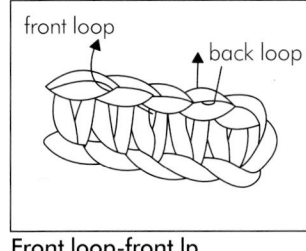

front loop

back loop

Front loop-front lp
Back Loop-back lp

Change colors

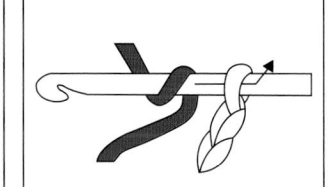

Change colors: drop first color; with 2nd color, pull through last lp of st.

Treble crochet

1

2

3

Treble crochet-tr: Yo twice, insert hook in st, yo, pull through st, [yo, pull through 2 lps] 3 times.

Double treble crochet

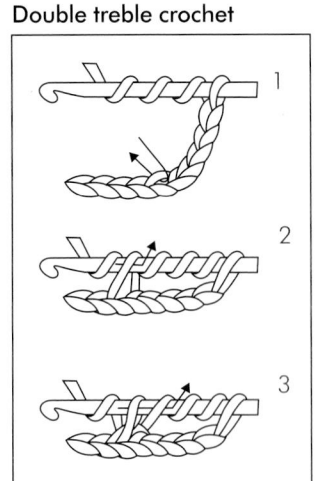

1

2

3

Double treble-dtr:
Yo 3 times, insert hook in st, yo, pull through st, [yo, pull through 2 lps] 4 times.

Stitch Guide

Single crochet decrease

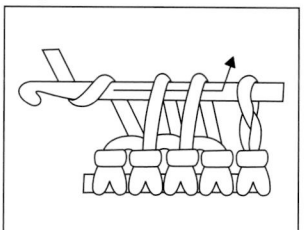

Single crochet decrease (sc dec): (insert hook, yo, draw lp through) in each of the sts indicated, yo, draw through all lps on hook.

CONVERSION CHART

U.S. TERM	U.K./AUS TERM
sl st slip st	**sc** single crochet
sc single crochet	**dc** double crochet
hdc half double crochet	**htr** half treble crochet
dc double crochet	**tr** treble crochet
tr treble crochet	**dtr** double treble crochet
dtr double treble crochet	**trip tr or trtr** triple treble crochet
yo yarn over	**yoh** yarn over hook

HEAD MEASURES

Measure around the head
Measure around the largest area, above the eyebrows to just above the ears and continuing across the back of the bend of the neck, and to the front of the head.

Measure front to back
Measure from just above the eyebrows, back over the crown, to the bend where the head meets the top of the neck.

Measure ear to ear
Measure at the top front of one ear, lay the tape measure up and over the crown to the same position on the other ear.

Size Chart–Babies (these are approx. measures)

Size (in months)	0-3	3-6	6-9	9-12
Head size	14"	16"	18"	19"

Size Chart–Child (these are approx. measures)

Size (in years)	2-4	5-8	9-12
Head size	19"	20"	21½"

Size Chart–Head size (these are approx. measures)

Teens	20½" - 22"
Women	21½" - 22½"
Men	23" - 24"

ABBREVIATIONS

beg. . . . . .begin	MC. . . . . . . .main color
CC. . . . .contrasting color	rep(s). . . . . . . .repeat(s)
ch(s). . . . . .chain(s)	rnd(s). . . . . . . .round(s)
ch sp(s). . . chain space(s)	sc. . . . . . .single crochet
cl(s). . . . . .cluster(s)	sc dec. . . single crochet 2 or more stitches together
cm. . . . . . .centimeter(s)	sk. . . . . .skip
dc. . . . . .double crochet	sl st(s). . . . .slip stitch(es)
dec. . . . . .decrease	st(s). . . . . .stitch(es)
dtr. . double treble crochet	tog. . . . . .together
hdc. . .half double crochet	tr. . . . . . . treble crochet
inc. . . . . .increase	yo. . . . . .yarn over
lp(s). . . . . .loop(s)	

Half double crochet decrease (hdc dec): (Yo, insert hook, yo, draw lp through) in each of the sts indicated, yo, draw through all lps on hook.

Double crochet decrease (dc dec): (Yo, insert hook, yo, draw loop through, yo, draw through 2 lps on hook) in each of the sts indicated, yo, draw through all lps on hook.

OUR MISSION

A portion of the author's proceeds from this book will be donated to a Fertility Chapter to help couples who need financial assistance to grow their families. Our mission is to assist couples who cannot afford fertility treatments, such as in vitro fertilization (IVF), that are not covered by health insurance, and with adoption.

COPYRIGHTS

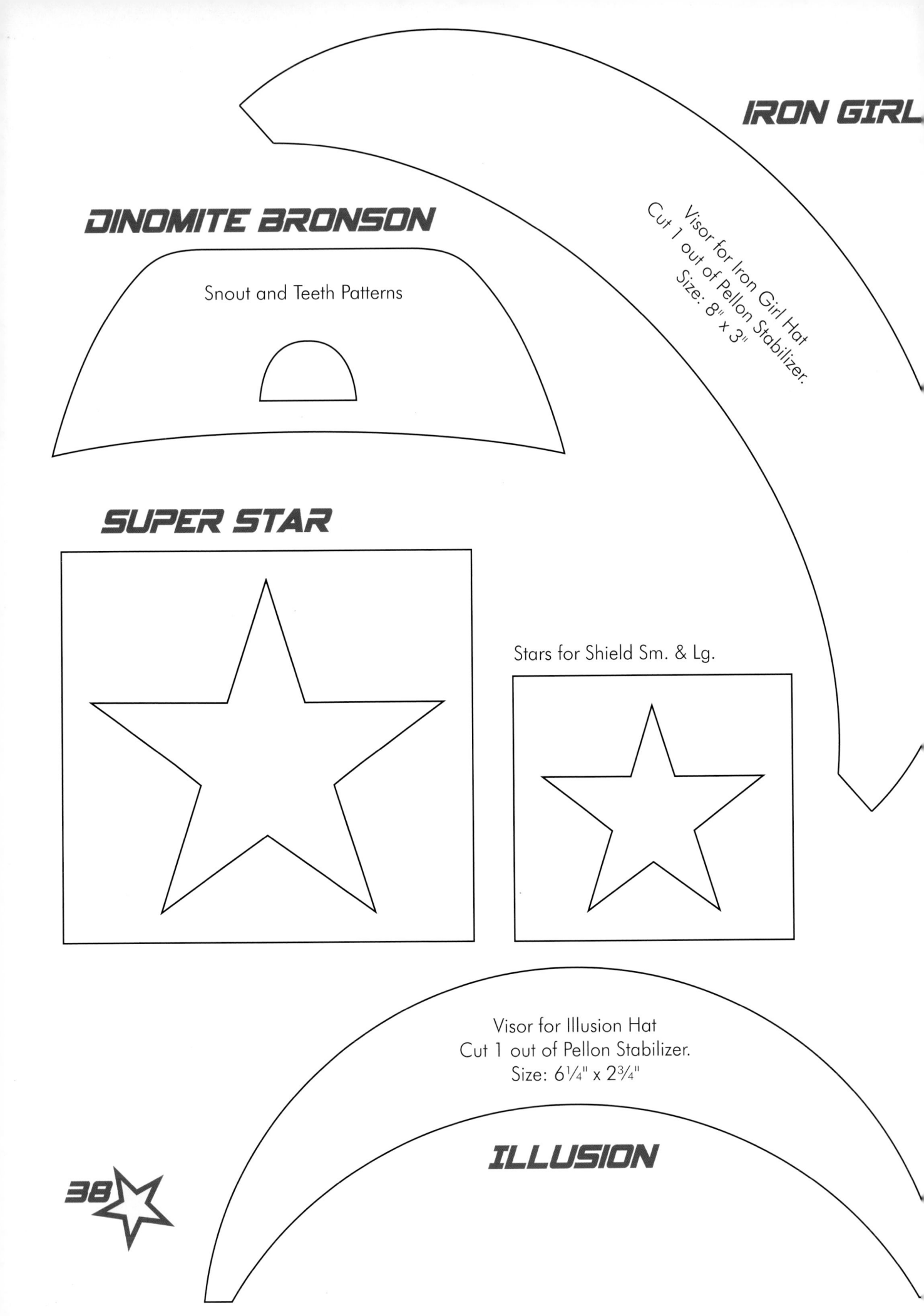

IRON GIRL

Visor for Iron Girl Hat
Cut 1 out of Pellon Stabilizer.
Size: 8" x 3"

DINOMITE BRONSON

Snout and Teeth Patterns

SUPER STAR

Stars for Shield Sm. & Lg.

Visor for Illusion Hat
Cut 1 out of Pellon Stabilizer.
Size: 6¼" x 2¾"

ILLUSION

38

Hat size: 18 diam.

Crown to edge: 7" height plus 1¼" cuff

Button eyes size: ¼"

Nose size: 1¼" x ¾"

Ears size: 1¾" w x 3⅜" h

Cut out along dotted lines. Place face pattern over hat. With fabric pen, trace mouth and nose onto hat. Embroider nose and mouth with running stitch.

FELINE HELIX

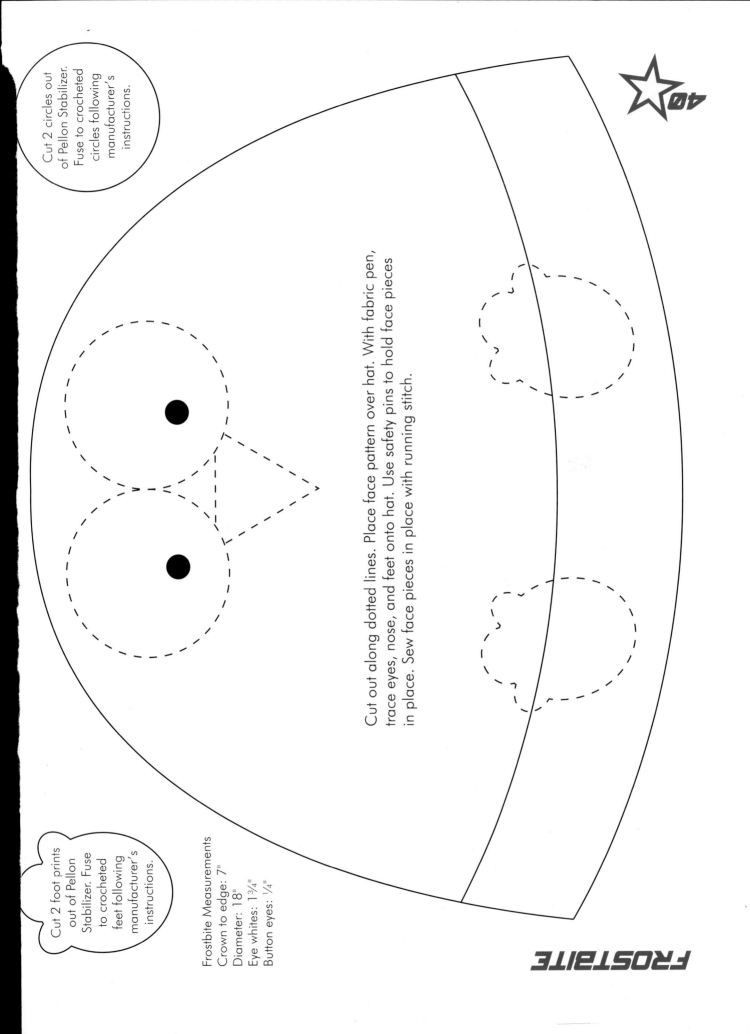

Cut 2 circles out of Pellon Stabilizer. Fuse to crocheted circles following manufacturer's instructions.

Cut out along dotted lines. Place face pattern over hat. With fabric pen, trace eyes, nose, and feet onto hat. Use safety pins to hold face pieces in place. Sew face pieces in place with running stitch.

Cut 2 foot prints out of Pellon Stabilizer. Fuse to crocheted feet following manufacturer's instructions.

Frostbite Measurements
Crown to edge: 7"
Diameter: 18"
Eye whites: 1¾"
Button eyes: ¼"

FROSTBITE